DESTINED

FOR GLORY

THE RACE TO RECEIVE THE CROWN

DEDO SUWANDA

THE TIME OF ACCELERATION IS HERE

DEDO SUWANDA

Copyright © 2024 by DEDO SUWANDA

Published by Book Writing Pioneer

Cover design by Book Writing Pioneer

ISBN: Printed in the United States

TABLE OF CONTENT

DEDO SUWANDA

FOREWORD

Born with a skeptical mind, I had a lot of questions, and I demanded and searched for answers to those questions. I thank God for giving me a sharp mind that enables me to search and find answers – to a certain limit. I understand now that God created everybody uniquely and dealt with everybody according to his unique personality. Due to my parents' pursuit of academic success, they sent me to the best schools in the city – which are usually Catholic schools or Christian schools. Therefore, I went to Catholic schools for the 12 years of elementary and secondary school education. I became a Catholic – baptized and went through all the sacraments – because that is all I knew as a young boy. I seriously learned the Catholic teachings, and started reading the Bible when I was in adolescence age. With passions in science and engineering, I started to notice inconsistencies between Catholic teaching, the Bible, and the intellectual teachings. I was blessed that I prospered in academic and career life in the early part of my life, but there were many unanswered questions to the inconsistencies.

At the age of 39, at the brink of mid-life, the need to get answers became more intense. Some suggested to me that faith is something that must be accepted despite a lack of understanding. It is true, but my heart was unsettled. I believe in God, and I have always been searching for Him and the truth about Him. Somehow, God sent me and my wife a business partner, also an intellectual but a believer in Christ, who helped us to come to the point of repentance. With a new fire inside me, I continued the pursuit of God, wanting to know everything about Him and His plan for my life. I started reading many books written by Christian authors and listened to teachings by Christian pastors and speakers. Unfortunately, I became more confused because everybody has a different take on Christianity, depending on his/her denomination. However, the Holy Spirit – the Spirit of wisdom and revelation – guided me to know the truth. He helped me by leading me to the people I should learn from, and He led me to understand the Bible as God intended it through the writers. Twenty-five years later, I arrive at the stage where I am now.

About ten years ago, I started to observe my fellow Christians who were ahead of me in receiving the grace of God through the faith of Christ. Many of them have been Christians for 20, 30, 40, and even 50 years, but they are either uninterested, unaware, or confused regarding the Gospel. Aren't they supposed to get closer to the "Promised Land", the "Rest" of God, but they are still wandering in circles in the wilderness of life, like Moses' generation of Israelites? They don't seem to go much farther than when they started the journey as a Christian. My heart was filled with sadness and compassion, and I decided to put aside some of my time and efforts to help them. God sent some to be taught and guided through mentorship, Bible Study, and sessions over lunch or coffee. I spent many hours in restaurants and coffee shops to speak to many Christians. I saw it as a ministry.

Two years after my born-again experience as a Christian, I was blessed with a prophetic ministry from God through a true New Covenant prophet, including God's desire for me and my wife to write books. This prophetic word has been confirmed at least twice in the past 20 years. Two years ago, I was reminded that the instruction to write books has been long overdue. One day at the beginning of 2024, God also reminded me of a prophetic word that He gave me in 2001 about another calling He has for me and my wife. For 2 months, I have been getting messages from at least 5 different Christian ministers that 2024 would be a time for that transition. I have been spending the majority of my time on business, and I have put ministry as a secondary priority. In March 2024, I made a decision to reverse that order. My wife and I went to Indonesia to explore ministry opportunities. As teaching is my highest passion and skill, we have been focussing on teaching opportunities. God has been gracious that several possibilities are opening for us – in Indonesia, Canada, and potentially other countries. After returning from the exploratory trip to Indonesia, I started writing this book, and four weeks later, the first draft was completed. God has inspired and enabled me to write the ideas on my laptop.

It has been my passion (I believe it is my calling) to see Christians grow to maturity. It is God's desire and plan that we all be transformed into the image of Christ from one level of glory to another level higher. God has predestined us to be glorified. I believe this book, and also my teaching materials, will help many Christians to understand the hope of glory from God and to have this hope manifested and fulfilled in their lifetime.

Amen!

INTRODUCTION

Talent shows, such as Britain's Got Talent (BGT) and America's Got Talent (AGT), have become very popular TV shows in the past two decades. I enjoy watching the shows - especially the auditions – when an unknown, shy, and nervous contestant starts to perform their debut in front of thousands of live audiences and millions of TV audiences. They put everything on the line and deliver the most amazing display of beauty and talent. I still remember the moment Susan Boyle, an awkward middle-aged woman in her out-of-fashion clothes and hairstyle, delivered an outstanding performance of "I Dream a Dream" from the musical "Les Miserables". She told Simon Cowel that her dream was she wanted to be like Elaine Paige, one of the greatest musical performers in London. The judges and many in the audience gave her a dismissal smirk, but they were struck with a big surprise when she opened her mouth and gave her a roaring applause – perhaps with a deep apology for their prejudice. People consider that moment as "glory revealed". Another great performer was Loren

Allred from BGT Season 15 in 2022. She was hired to train Rebecca Ferguson, who played the role of Jenny Lind in the very successful movie "The Greatest Showman" (2017), but she was chosen to be the playback singer of Jenny Lind for the commercially successful song "Never Enough". For years, not many people knew Loren Allred until she revealed her identity as the true voice of Jenny Lind at the BGT audition in 2022. She sang beautifully at that audition, and the judges and over 4000 live audiences, plus millions of TV audiences, were wowed by her performance that night. When I saw those performances on the TV screen, one thought came through my mind – what a "glory"!

On July 13, 2024, the leading candidate of the US Election 2024, former President Donald J. Trump, was in his last campaign before the RNC Convention. A few minutes into his campaign speech, he ducked and hid behind the podium on the stage because several bullets were flying in his direction. The secret service agents ran towards him and provided protection for him. There was chaos and uncertainties about what had just happened. A few moments later, he was escorted out of the podium – after the Secret Service agents received confirmation that the shooter had been neutralized. Twice – on the way to the presidential limousine – Trump forced himself out of the protective embrace of the secret service agents so that he could lift his fist and yell, "Fight, fight, fight". A photographer from AP (Associated Press) managed to capture that moment – *a glorious moment.* With the US flags spread behind him and surrounded by the secret service agents, Trump, with blood on his ear and cheek and with his fist up in the air, rose above the people around him and shouted: "Fight, fight, fight". This glorious moment will be remembered by people around the world forever. It is a picture of a glorious moment.

There were events in my life when I was blessed enough to see the natural beauty of God's creation. When I was in high school, I saw an almost perfect half-circle rainbow in a bright sky. I experienced a glorious sunset in Kuta Beach, Bali, Indonesia. Recently, I was at the feet of Mount Sewu in Central Java, staring up at the mountain top on a clear day. Two years ago, I took my uncle to Niagara Falls to see one of the seven wonders of the world. It was his first time to see Niagara Falls from the Canadian side, which is better than the view from the USA side. He pointed out to me the greatness of God in creating such a magnificent wonder. I have seen – in photos and videos - many more wonders and natural beauty around the world. No wonder the apostle Paul wrote in the Book of Romans, *"They know the truth about God because He has made it obvious to them. For ever since the world was created, people have seen the earth and sky. Through everything God made, they can clearly see His invisible qualities—His eternal power and divine nature. So they have no excuse for not knowing God."* The reflection of the glory of God can be seen in all God's creation.

What is the Glory of God?

In our modern time, the word "glory" is often misused and even downgraded. It is often used to describe something wonderful, amazing, or beautiful. However, "glory" is a word that we, Christian believers, should only use to describe God only. We say God is glorious. The Bible declares that He is – but you cannot accurately and fully describe it in words. The word "glory" is recorded over 600 times in the Bible. It depicts worth and value, but it also refers to the greatness of God. I would like to describe "glory" as the very nature of God – His attributes (characters) and His greatness (wisdom and power). It is the very presence of God.

There are many theologians and Bible experts who spoke and wrote about the subject. God declared His name to different people of God throughout the ages. Moses wrote the word *"Elohim" (plural form)*, or *"God"* in the English language when he wrote the Book of Genesis. This word was used over 2300 times in the Bible. It means the "Creator of the heavens and the earth". Another name that was used often (over 6500 times) is *"YHWH"*. The English translation is *"LORD"*. The Jews considered the word *YHWH* too sacred to be spoken, so they intentionally did not preserve the pronunciation. Today, no one knows exactly how it was supposed to be pronounced. The meaning is similar to the meaning of *"I AM"*, the name He declared to Moses at the burning bush. Its basic

9

meaning is *"The Self-Existing One"* or *"The Eternal"* or *"the Alpha and Omega"*. It emphasizes that God has lived for eternity—He had no beginning and will have no end. He was not brought into existence at any point in history by any other being—He is self-existent. The term *YHWH* is often used in conjunction with another description: *"YHWH Rapha"* (The LORD who Heals), *"YHWH Jirah"* (THE LORD provides), *"YHWH Tsidkenu"* (The LORD Our Righteousness), *"YHWH Shalom"* (The LORD Our Peace), "YHWH Nissi" (The LORD My Banner or Protector), and many more. However, the New Testament gave more intimate and relational names that the Old Testament people did not know and experience. God is *"LOVE"* (1 John 4:8). This is who He is. God is our FATHER. Jesus is *"THE WORD"*, *"MESSIAH"* or *"CHRIST" (The Anointed One)*, *IMMANUEL (God With Us)*, *our "SHEPHERD"* and our "SAVIOUR", but He is also our *FIRSTBORN BROTHER*, our *"JOINT-HEIR"*, our *INTERCESSOR (Stand In Between)* and our *BRIDEGROOM*. The Holy Spirit is our *HELPER (Gk. parakletos)*, our *COMFORTER*, and our *FRIEND*. There are many more names that are attached to God than we can describe with words.

Am I downgrading the true meaning of glory to describe the moment of Susan Boyle's audition performance at BGT in 2009? Perhaps not! *Genesis 1:27* says, ***"So God created man in his own image, in the image of God He created him; male and female He*** *created them."* Despite the fall of Adam and Eve, the image of God, including His glory, remained, though somewhat covered and blurred. However, after the completed works of Christ at the cross, those who decide to receive His faith and grace are restored – even better than the condition of Adam at the time of creation. The restoration of the image of God in humans, including the imparted glory has been restored.

The Glory Restrained in the Old Testament

In the Old Testament, Moses said, **"Please show me your glory."** *(Exodus 33:18).* He really desired to see the glory of God. God responded that He would show His goodness and compassion to Moses; however," He said, *"You cannot see my face, for man shall not see me and live."* Moses, a prophet, a teacher, a leader, the writer of the first five books, and the greatest hero of the Old Testament, was not allowed to see the glory of God. Moses went up to Mount Sinai to speak with God. God gave him the Ten Commandments and showed him the pattern of the Tabernacle in heaven so that he could create a duplicate on earth. However, he was only allowed to see the back of God. The holiness of God was too sacred even to the man with the greatest faith in the Old Testament.

DESTINED FOR GLORY

The Glory of God Revealed in the New Testament

Peter, James, and John experienced the glory of Jesus Christ personally at the Mount of Transfiguration. In the Gospel of Matthew, he described Jesus' face shone like the sun, and his clothes became as white as light. However, the Apostle Paul told us to behold or see the glory of the Lord as in a mirror. How can this happen? We don't see Jesus appearing daily with His face shiny like the sun and His clothes white as light. How can we see the glory of the Lord Jesus on a daily basis? This is a subject to be presented in Chapter 2.

The good news is Jesus came and died for our sins, overcame death with glorious victory, and was resurrected to give us His righteousness. The Good News did not stop there but included the restoration of mankind to the original design and plan of God at the beginning, and even better. Our relationship with the Father, Jesus Christ, and the Holy Spirit is more relational now – based on the names He gave to the New Testament believers. Jesus has revealed to us who God is. Jesus said, *"And he who sees Me sees Him who sent Me." (John 12:45)* and *"If you had known Me, you would have known My Father also; and from now on you know Him and have seen Him." (John 14:7)* If we believe and receive His offer, we will not only see the glory of God through Jesus Christ, but His glory will also arise in us. We are destined to have His glory in us. I am blessed and grateful that I live under the New Covenant.

CHAPTER 1

THE FUTURE GLORY OF THE CHURCH

Arise, shine, for your light has come,

and the glory of the Lord has risen upon you.

For behold, darkness shall cover the earth,

and thick darkness the peoples;

but the Lord will arise upon you,

and His glory will be seen upon you.

And nations shall come to your light,

and kings to the brightness of your rising.

Lift up your eyes all around, and see;

DEDO SUWANDA

they all gather together, they come to you;

your sons shall come from afar,

and your daughters shall be carried on the hip.

Then you shall see and be radiant;

your heart shall thrill and exult,

because the abundance of the sea shall be turned to you,

the wealth of the nations shall come to you.

A multitude of camels shall cover you,

the young camels of Midian and Ephah;

all those from Sheba shall come.

They shall bring gold and frankincense,

and shall bring good news, the praises of the Lord.

All the flocks of Kedar shall be gathered to you;

the rams of Nebaioth shall minister to you;

they shall come up with acceptance on my altar,

and I (God) will beautify my beautiful house. (Isaiah 60:1-7)

I love the Book of Isaiah. It is an Old Testament book, but it speaks much of New Testament content. A Bible scholar pointed out the similarity between the Bible and the Book of Isaiah. The Bible contains sixty-six books, with thirty-nine Old Testament and twenty-seven New Testament books. The Book of Isaiah has sixty-six chapters, with thirty-nine chapters aligned to the Old Testament and twenty-seven chapters containing New Testament prophecies. Many prophecies about Jesus Christ, His works on the cross and the "grace age" are found in the last twenty-seven chapters of the Book of Isaiah. For example, Isaiah 53 contains a prophecy of the Atonement of Jesus Christ. Isaiah prophesied that the Savior would be despised and rejected, smitten and afflicted, that He would carry our sorrows, and that He would be wounded for our transgressions. Isaiah 54 (with a title added by the translator, *"The New Covenant of Peace"*) describes the New Covenant under which the believers in Christ are living. Jesus, in his first official ministry in a synagogue in Nazareth, reading from Isaiah 61, declared that He was the Anointed One (the Messiah), and He was appointed to liberate the oppressed and help the poor (Luke 4).

Let us now look at the 60th chapter of the Book of Isaiah. I have always been fascinated by this Scripture and hoped that this prophecy would be fulfilled in my lifetime. Some Bible scholars argue that Isaiah 60 pertains the future of the nation of Israel due to the reference to Jacob (and as the title *"The Future Glory of Isarel"* indicates, which was added by the English translator of the Bible). Others believe that Isaiah 60 is a prophecy about the Millenium

Kingdom of *Revelation 20*, while others consider it as a prophecy of the *"New Jerusalem of Revelation 20 and 21"* because of the reference in *Revelation 20:19, "The sun shall be no more your light by day, nor for brightness shall the moon give you light; but the LORD will be your everlasting light, and your God will be your glory"*. Based on the principle of *"Duality of Biblical Prophecy"*, Isaiah 60 is both a picture of "Natural Israel" in the future and a picture of "Spiritual Israel", which is the current Church of Jesus Christ that has been in existence for 2000 years. I, therefore, believe that Isaiah 60 is the prophecy about the Church, the Bride of Christ.

What Time Is It Now?

I believe we are living in an unprecedented time, at least in over six decades of my life. We have seen wars and tribulations, such as pandemics, inflation, and depression, in the world. The COVID-19 pandemic, which started in 2020, brought a lot of changes in the way people live and behave worldwide. Millions of people died of pandemics in the past, but I am sensing something is different this time, despite the lower human casualty of COVID-19. It is something spiritual. My spirit can sense it, but my mind cannot explain or rationalize it. I am also sensing a so-called "dark cloud" moving in this world we are living in. What was in disguise for centuries is now being revealed. A certain elite group of people, people would call it the Globalist with the One Government agenda, is increasing its efforts to dominate all aspects of life, health care, food supplies, energy, environment, education, information, social norms, and most of all, finances. This elite group strongly pushed its tagline, *"You will own nothing and be happy"*. I wonder how many people actually believe it, except the desperate ones who are deceived into believing that there are no other alternatives. With the advance of information technology, social media, and, most importantly, artificial intelligence, the severity of the phenomena seems to be accelerating. Many believe that such acceleration will be out of control – at least for most commoners outside the elite group. Is this a fulfillment of the prophecy *"For behold, darkness shall cover the earth, and thick darkness the peoples"*?

We have also observed the situation in the world. There had not been many physical wars nor millions of casualties of war as in the previous World Wars, except the war in Ukraine that had killed about 500,000 people as of July 2024. The war between Russia and Ukraine, which is a proxy of NATO, including the United States of America, is unnecessary and seems like it was intentionally created for the benefit of certain people. With the rise of Trump in the USA and the defeat of the war hawk leaders of the European Union (EU), the war between Ukraine and Russia will hopefully come to a halt – at least temporarily. Similarly, the threat of war in the Middle East, started by the deadliest attack on Israel since the Holocaust by Hamas on October 7, 2023, may be defused soon.

There are uncertainties in our current world. *"Darkness seems to cover the earth, and thick darkness seems to cover the people".* However, it is not yet the time of the *"Great Tribulation"* as described in the *Book of Revelation.* The Devil may try to accelerate such fulfillment, but the Almighty God is in full control (it will be addressed later in this chapter). The Devil can only respond to the "Great Move of God" in the time of acceleration. God's plan always prevails!

Should we worry?

Many people don't think so because they do not discern but only use their natural eyes and thoughts. Those who have more accurate "information" do worry but feel helpless and hope only for the best. Unfortunately, many Christians are in the camp of the two groups of people mentioned above. They call themselves Christians, but they think and act like the unbelievers, i.e., the rest of the world's population. Note that I will use the terms *"we"* and *"us"* to describe the believers in Christ or the church. Jesus told us that *"we are not of the world, just as Jesus is not"*, and Jesus asked the Father, *"I do not ask that You take them out of the world, but that You keep them from the evil one."* Jesus assured us that God will ensure that we are not subjected to the evil one. It is a wonderful promise. The apostle Paul also reminded us that *"we are more than a conqueror though Jesus Christ" (Romans 8:37)* and we can *"reign in life"* because we have *"received the abundance of grace and the free gift of righteousness" (Romans 5:17).* The truth is Christ has sent us to be *"ambassadors"* on earth to represent the Kingdom of God whose dominion includes the earth. It is reassuring to know that an ambassador is not subject to the law and authority of the country he is sent to. Unfortunately, many Christians are unaware or ignorant of the truth, and some who have been informed decide not to believe the truth about God's promises. Even those who are informed and believe are often forgetful; thus, they panic when they see with their natural eyes the coming "dark cloud," forgetting that our God is still in full control.

Let us explore further what the "truth" that the Word of God says about who we are. We have become sons (and daughters) who are loved by our Father and own the rights to the inheritance. We are called *"joint heir"* with Christ. The Father says to His son, *"Son, you are always with me, and all that is mine is yours." (Luke 15:31),* and He has declared, *"The silver is mine, and the gold is mine" (Haggai 2:8).* Really? Does all the wealth of the world belong to us? Let me take you to the deeper truth about our identity. Jesus calls us His friends, **"You are my friends if you do what I command. I no longer call you servants because a servant does not know his master's business. Instead, I have called you friends, for everything that I learned from my Father I have made known to you." *(John 15:14-15)*** Jesus has made known to us everything that

He knows. He also says, ***"Greater love has no one than this: to lay down one's life for one's friends."*** *(John 15:13)* Wow! What an honor and privilege!

God had a better and bigger plan when He created mankind. Let me take you to the next and highest level. The story of Abraham sending Eliezer, his most trusted servant, to find a wife for his son Isaac is a picture of the Father sending the Holy Spirit to find a bride for the Son, Jesus Christ. The Church is called the *"bride of Christ"*. There is no relationship more intimate than the relationship between a husband and a wife. The story of *"The King Who Loved A Humble Maiden"* by Soren Kierkegaard tells us the love story between Jesus, the *"King"*, and us, the *"humble maiden"*. The king left the kingdom and took a new identity as a poor commoner so that he could be with her and know if she loved him as a person – not out of fear of the king or out of the desire for his status or wealth. Jesus loves us and desires us to love Him back as a person, as a "husband". King Solomon perfectly describes the relationship between Christ and His bride in the *"Book of Song of Songs"*. Do you want to see how Jesus sees His Bride? Jesus, the King, says to the bride, *"Behold, you are beautiful, my love, behold, you are beautiful! Your eyes are doves behind your veil. ... You are altogether beautiful, my love; there is no flaw in you. ... You have captivated my heart, my sister, my bride; you have captivated my heart with one glance of your eyes, with one jewel of your necklace. How beautiful is your love, my sister, my bride! How much better is your love than wine and the fragrance of your oils than any spice!"* Jesus sees us as beautiful and flawless. Really? How about our sins, our adulterous acts, and our betrayals? How can Jesus' heart be captivated by us, who see ourselves as ugly and dark, and say, *"I am very dark, but lovely, O daughters of Jerusalem, like the tents of Kedar, like the curtains of Solomon. Do not gaze at me because I am dark, because the sun has looked upon me."* Jesus always sees us as beautiful, flawless, and captivating. The only thing Jesus would like to hear from the bride is, *"I am my beloved's, and His desire is for me. Come, my beloved, let us go out into the fields and lodge in the villages; let us go out early to the vineyards and see whether the vines have budded, whether the grape blossoms have opened, and the pomegranates are in bloom. There, I will give You my love."*

We have seen the romantic part of the relationship between the King and his bride. However, the King has seen the bride with inherent glory because Jesus, who is not bound by time and space can see to the future. The bride is destined for her true identity – a glorious bride. Let us see the story of Queen Esther, who is the bride of King Ahasuerus. Years after becoming a queen, Esther often forgot her true identity – the wealth, power, and authority – a queen to the most powerful king of her time. When the former prime minister, Haman, issued an edict that all Jews throughout the kingdom territory were to be killed, she panicked and felt helpless.

This was despite the fact that Haman had been defeated and hung to death. She went to the king and begged the king to help her and do something about it. The king's answer was surprising yet full of truth. *"Behold, I have given Esther the house of Haman, and they have hanged him on the gallows because he intended to lay hands on the Jews. but you may write as you please with regard to the Jews, in the name of the king, and seal it with the king's ring, for an edict written in the name of the king and sealed with the king's ring cannot be revoked."* *(Esther 8:7-8)* Prior to this event, the king had told Esther that half of the kingdom was already hers. The king had also given Esther Haman's position as the Prime Minister, which was the second highest position in the kingdom, and the authority and power to declare edicts and rule the nation. Esther forgot her status, her position, and her authority as a queen. It is saddening that most Christians are not aware of nor believe in the position, authority, and power they already have in this world. We come to God begging Him for crumbs while God has given us half of His kingdom, including the wealth, the authority, and the power of the Kingdom.

The Grand Master of Chess

We are back to the question, "Should we worry?" Yes, the world is getting darker, and the people are covered by deep darkness. What should be our response? Without understanding the "truth" about the reason and the result of the work of Christ at the cross, many sincere Christians think that the evil one has the upper hand and God is playing catch-up as if Satan is the master of the universe. The truth is that God is the Almighty, the Omni-presence (present in all space), the Omni-science (knowing all) God, and the God with all His glory, power, and dominion. Satan is just a created angel who has been thrown away from heaven, defeated for the second time by Christ in Sheol, and has been disarmed completely. His only weapons are deception, schemes, and accusations to sidetrack us. We have also been equipped with the armours of God to defend the victory and the territory that we have been given by Jesus Christ. Satan is not all-knowing and all-present, and he has been fully stripped of his prior power. Therefore, when we see the moves of the enemy, we can be certain that he is the one responding to the move of God, not the other way around. As a Grand Master, God is in control of the Chess Game, and we know the end results. When you see those "scary" circumstances in this world with all the bad news, I would encourage you to ask God to give you the gifts of discernment and wisdom to perceive and understand what God is doing. God has enlightened your spiritual eyes so that you can perceive what is happening in the spiritual realm. Having the perception and the perspective of God is important to live and walk in the visual world we live in. What is seen in plain sight is *"temporal"* or *"earthly"* in nature, but what cannot be seen with our natural eyes but can be seen with our spiritual eyes are *"eternal"* and *"heavenly"*.

The Bible clearly tells us that Satan, or Lucifer, is a defeated angel. Make no mistake - Lucifer is real and was a powerful being, but he is also only a created being. The Book of Ezekiel describes him like this, ***"You were the signet of perfection, full of wisdom and perfect in beauty. … On the day that you were created, they were prepared. You were an anointed guardian cherub. I (God) placed you; you were on the holy mountain of God; in the midst of the stones of fire you walked. You were blameless in your ways from the day you were created till unrighteousness was found in you. …Your heart was proud because of your beauty; you corrupted your wisdom for the sake of your splendor. I cast you to the ground …"*** *(Ezekiel 28:12-17)* What fault did Lucifer do? His heart became prideful. There are thousands of different kinds of sins, but pride is the source of all sins, and God hates pride more than any other sin. What did this pride lead to?

The Book of Isaiah describes, ***"How you are fallen from heaven, O Day Star (Lucifer), son of Dawn! How you are cut down to the ground, you who laid the nations low! You said in your heart, 'I will ascend to heaven; above the stars of God, I will set my throne on high; I will sit on the mount of assembly in the far reaches of the north; I will ascend above the heights of the clouds; I will make myself like the Most High."*** *(Isaiah 14:12-14)* Pride leads to rebellion and the desire to replace God and be independent of God. The recent developments in the world, the advancement of technology and artificial intelligence (AI), enable mankind to achieve such wicked desires. Noah Yuval Harari, an Israeli scholar with high influence in the World Economic Forum, declared that he would write a "new" Bible using AI that would be more accepted by people than the "true" Bible. He also declares that people are now hackable and can be controlled. We also see how a few rich people who control a huge portion of the wealth of the world through venture capital firms, such as BlackRock, Vanguard, and State Street, think that they can rule the world.

Did God lose control of the universe He created? By no means! The Book of Revelation says, ***"Now war arose in heaven, Michael and his angels fighting against the dragon. And the dragon and his angels fought back, but he was defeated, and there was no longer any place for them in heaven. And the great dragon was thrown down, that ancient serpent, who is called the devil and Satan, the deceiver of the whole world—he was thrown down to the earth, and his angels were thrown down with him."*** *(Revelation 12:7-9)* This is the first of many defeats Satan experienced and will experience again. The first defeat took place long before Adam and Eve were created. Satan and all the fallen angels were thrown away from heaven to the earth. What? To the earth? I used to wonder why God threw Satan and all his followers to the earth – a place where

God created men and all the good things, such as plants and animals. Why did God put men on the "same" earth where evil exists? You know the rest of the story. Men fell to sin through Satan's deception – the same deception that brought Satan down, which is pride and the desire to be like God. Satan was able to take control of the dominion and authority over all creation from men. It is tragic! I wished Adam and Eve were wiser and less prideful. However, God had planned for the redemption of mankind through Jesus Christ.

Satan dominated the world, with the exception of God's chosen people of Israel, until Jesus came to the earth and completed the task. His assignment was to save and redeem the world through His victory by death and resurrection. At the depth of Sheol, Jesus defeated Satan for the second time. Jesus also defeated death, curses, bondages and shame – and the victory is now available for anyone who believes and is willing to receive His grace by faith. Note that the Bible prophesied that Satan would be defeated again – for the third time - at the Battle of Armageddon at the end of the Great Tribulation period. He will be bound for one thousand years, but God will release him for a short period of time at the end of the Millennium. Satan will try to deceive people again, but he will be defeated for the fourth and last time, and he will thrown into the lake of fire forever.

As for us, the believers in Christ, during the Age of Grace, we must know that Satan is a defeated being, and he has no power, dominion, or control over the people of God. The "only" weapon and influence he can exercise on us is deception, accusation, and condemnation. Our spiritual warfare is "not" to achieve victory (which has been completed by Christ and given to us) but to "stand firm" and "defend" the territory that has been given to us. The spiritual armour of God is the Truth, the Righteousness, the Gospel of Peace, Salvation, Faith, and the Word of God – which are all about Christ and His free gift for us. Also, "praying at all times in the Spirit" is added to complete the armours of God for our warfare. Knowing our position in Christ and the weapons required to defend our victory is the key principle in living a victorious life. The apostle Paul summed up in *Romans 5:17* that the key to *"reigning in life"* is "receiving the abundance (hyper) of grace and the free gift of *righteousness"*. The "Grand Master of Chess" has restored and delegated the dominion and authority to us, the believers in Christ, and has taught us to reign in life. It is our part to learn to know our identity in Christ, the "beloved" bride with dominion and power to live a victorious life and learn to mature so that we can walk in the calling and purpose we have been destined for. We have been destined for glory!

The Glory of The Lord Will Be Seen in Us

Isaiah 60 starts with an instruction to us to *"arise and shine"*. I am puzzled by the fact that many Christians do not have the confidence to arise and shine. They don't look different from the rest of the people of the world. The Scripture is clear regarding the reason why we should arise and shine – because the glory of the Lord *"has"* risen upon us. Note that the word "has"! This phenomenon started 2000 years ago after the coming of the Holy Spirit on the day of Pentecost. If you don't believe me, read again the Book of Acts, which is proof that Isaiah 60 is a prophecy for the Church. It is true that the Church has experienced the *"Dark Ages"* for over 1000 years since the adoption of Christian practice by Caesar Constantine in the 4th century. Martin Luther rekindled true Christianity, followed by the revival in England, and finally, with the spiritual awakening in the USA in the 20th century. We have seen the growth of Christianity since the Reformation in 1527, and Christianity has grown exponentially in the 20th century. Despite the growth, the true "born-again" Christians are only about 11 percent of the world's population by the end of the 20th century.

Despite the "mediocre" visible growth thus far, I am extremely confident of the truth and the fulfillment of the prophecy of God. I believe we are in the era of acceleration. We are in a period called the *"End Time"*. We are in the period of the "Latter Rain" of *Zechariah 10*. The *"Latter Glory"* of the House of God will be greater than the *"Former Glory" (Haggai 2:9)*. I believe the church, and every member of the church, every "living stones", is the "eternal dwelling place or temple of God". It will be glorious and bright. The glory of the Lord and the light of God will be so visible in the Church that *"nations will come to its light"* and *"kings will come to its brightness"*. Nations are the people of the world, we often refer to as unbelievers, and kings are their leaders in governments, businesses and all other organizations. The term "Seven Mountains", which visions were received almost simultaneously by Bill Bright, the founder of Campus Crusade, and Loren Cunningham, the founder of Youth With A Mission (YWAM), in the 1980s. When nations and their kings come to the Church voluntarily and eagerly, it is because they see the glory of the Lord and the light of God in us. Evangelization efforts and missions will be very easy. I am imagining the fulfillment of the prophecy of the Great Harvest. Hard work and burdensome financial requirements will not be required because nations and their kings will come voluntarily when they see the glory of the Lord and the light of God. I long to see this picture – in my lifetime.

The Great Wealth Transfer Prophecy

Isaiah 60 starts with God giving an instruction for His people to *"arise and shine"* so that the glory and the light of God are visible to attract nations and kings. His next instruction is for us to *"lift our eyes all around and see"*. He wants us to observe what God is about to do. This reminds me of the story of Elijah *(1 Kings 18:41-46)* when he was told by God to return to the evil king Ahab and announce the end of a drought that had lasted for more than three years. Elijah told King Ahab, *"Go up, eat and drink; for there is a sound of abundance of rain."* Then Elijah went up to the top of Mount Carmel, bowed down on the ground, and put his face between his knees to pray. He told his servant to look towards the sea and see if the rain is coming. This was repeated seven times. At the seventh time, his servant said, *"There is a cloud as a man's hand, rising out of the sea!"* Elijah immediately told Ahab to prepare the chariot and warned him to go down before the rain stopped him. Immediately, the sky became black with clouds and wind, and there was a heavy rain.

Elijah believed the word of God, but the fulfillment took some time. He repeatedly observed the sky, the natural realm, expecting the fulfillment of the promise. Upon seeing a small cloud the size of a man's hand, he believed the heavy rain would come, and he took action by faith. I am seeing a *"small cloud"* from the signs in the physical realm that the time of acceleration is starting already. I believe the *"heavy rain"* will come soon. I have *"lifted my eyes all around, and saw"* and *"my heart would thrill and exult"*. What is the reason for the excitement? *"Because the abundance of the sea shall be turned to you, the wealth of the nations shall come to you."* It is amazing! Not only nations and their kings will come to us, and most likely, they will come back to the Lord through us, they will bring their wealth to us for the kingdom of God. The word *"sea"* is referring to the world – the secular or pagan world. The abundance of the pagan world will be turned to us, the church. The wealth of the nations and their kings' wealth will be turned to us. It is the "wealth transfer" from the world or the "unrighteous", to the church, who are the "righteous". *(Proverbs 13:22)*

How God Sees Wealth

God is the owner of everything in the whole universe. The gold and silver are His. The cattle in the thousand hills are His. In the current time, all the money in the banks is His. All the buildings the infrastructure, such as roads, bridges, power plants, airports, and many more, are His. All the stocks, bonds, and financial papers are his. All the factories, the mines, and the farms in the world are his. In his book "The Great Wealth Transfer", Peter Youngren started by explaining that God's most precious wealth is people whom He loved very much from the beginning. As mentioned above, all creations, including financial and industrial wealth, are also His. He then also explained, in breadth and depth, the subject of the Financial Wealth Transfer historically and prophetically. He also explained God's purpose for all wealth transfers from the unrighteous to the righteous people. Two wealth transfers have happened in the past – in the Old Testament. Every wealth transfer was arranged by God Himself for the purpose of building the *"Dwelling Place of God"*. The first wealth transfer happened 1500 years before Jesus Christ came to the world. After 430 years of slavery in Egypt, God appointed Moses to deliver the Israelites, take them out of Egypt as free people, and lead them to the land that God promised their "father", Abraham. Through Moses, God instructed the Israelites to ask, or demand, every household in Egypt to give them precious things, including gold and silver. After the deliverance at Passover, the Pharaoh allowed them to leave (but he changed his mind later). Just before they left Egypt, they did what God instructed them to do, and they received all the gold, silver, and other precious things. The Egyptians gladly gave them the precious things because they were happy to see the Israelites leave their countries after the Egyptians experienced the Ten Plagues, especially the death of their eldest sons. The loot was like an outstanding payment to them working as slaves for over 400 years. A more detailed discussion on the matter of Wealth Transfer, especially the future Wealth Transfer of the New Testament, will be presented in Chapter 5.

The most important question is, *"What is the purpose of the wealth?"* If you examine the Book of Exodus in chapters 25 to 28, God instructed Moses and the people of Israel to build a tabernacle based on a design of the real tabernacle that Moses saw in heaven with every single item seen in the Heavenly Tabernacle, and the procedures of conducting ceremonies and offerings. The Tabernacle built by the Israelites was a *"dwelling place of God"* among His people. God delights Himself to be among His people. God's presence will be with the Israelites during their journey in the wilderness, on the way to the Promised Land. The Tabernacle and all its elements were made of gold, silver and other precious materials that the Israelites got from the spoil. The ceremonies and offerings require expensive ingredients and animals. Considering the Israelites had been slaves for the past 400 years in Egypt (slaves dis not earn wages, except for simple and basic necessities for life), how could they build the extravagant dwelling place of God and the expensive ingredients needed for the ceremonies and offerings? God provided all they needed for His purpose and glory. This is the purpose of the wealth that God ensures us through His provision. Further discussion will be presented in Chapter 6.

DEDO SUWANDA

CHAPTER 2

THE INCREASE OF GLORY IN THE CHURCH

God's Original Intention with Men and Women

God the Trinity, who is the Father, the Son, and the Holy Spirit, has no beginning and no end. God is love, and the Trinity has always been in a perfect love relationship with each other. Long before God created any living creatures on earth, including Adam and Eve, God created angels (meaning "messengers") with different ranks and tasks to serve Him. One of the archangels, the wisest and the most beautiful one, Lucifer, was filled with pride and desire to be like God. God sent the warrior archangel, Michael, to defeat him and send him out of heaven, to the earth.

When we read the Book of Genesis about *"Creation"* without understanding the prior events, we will be lost. It is like missing the first twenty minutes of the movie, and we are unaware of the characters in the story. The first chapter of the Book of Genesis tells the story of God creating something "new", starting by transforming the dark and formless earth into a beautiful place with perfect order between darkness and light, land and water, all the plants and animals in the air, in the water and on the earth. On the sixth day, the last day of "Creation", when every *"good"* thing has been created, God created men – male and female. God called them *"very good"*. Unlike the angels and the animals, men were created in the image and likeness of the Trinity God, including His glory. In fact, God created men out of the abundance and overflowing love among the Trinity. God created men with specific purposes: God wanted them to be fruitful, to multiply, to fill the whole earth, and to have dominion over all creation – on His behalf. What a beautiful plan of God!

Then God said, **"LET US MAKE MAN IN OUR IMAGE, ACCORDING TO OUR LIKENESS; LET THEM HAVE DOMINION OVER THE FISH OF THE SEA, OVER THE BIRDS OF THE AIR, and ... SO GOD CREATED MAN IN HIS OWN IMAGE; IN THE IMAGE OF GOD HE CREATED HIM; MALE AND FEMALE HE CREATED THEM. Then God blessed them, and God said to them, "Be fruitful and multiply; fill the** *earth and subdue it; have dominion over the fish of the sea, over the birds of the air, and over every living thing that moves on the earth." (Genesis 1:26-28)*

Lucifer, who is called the Devil or Satan after his fall from heaven, was jealous. He did not like God's plan with men. He tried to ruin the plan of God from the day of "Creation". He did not have power over men, but he used his deception and craftiness to make men lose their dominion. Using their free will, men decided to accept and believe the "half-truth" deception and fell to sin. The term "half-truth" simply means that Satan does not usually offer blatant lies but twists the truth that is attractive to the mind and the heart of men. Men, Adam and Eve, subsequently lost the glory of God in them and, with it, the dominion over the earth. Satan took over the dominion over the creation, and since the "Fall", the Devil ruled the earth using the "stolen" authority and power.

Unlike the Devil and his fallen angels, God immediately started a rescue plan through His Son, Jesus Christ. God had never abandoned His love towards men and had never left them. However, how could God bring men back into a loving relationship with Him? The rescue plan involved the Father sending the Son to become a "man", a perfect man, to redeem and restore men to the original state – and even better. Somebody had to die and shed His blood for the forgiveness of sin and to restore the original plan of God. The Son must come to the earth as man, representing all men, for redemption.

Unlike Adam, the restored men have become a *"new creation" (2 Corinthians 5:17)*. Because of His love, God offered men a "full-fledged" restoration and called all to be "conformed" to the image of the Son of God, again, with the fullness of His glory. All men have been offered "justification" (or "righteousness of God") and "glorification" ("to be filled with glory"), but the transformation will happen only to those who are willing to believe and receive His offer. Believing simply means receiving the offer from God" by grace through faith". Grace, the undeserved favour of God," is offered to all of us. Jesus also created faith and offered His faith to all of us. If we decide to accept His faith, we will have the ability to believe and receive His grace for forgiveness of sin and for restoration to a new creation. Without going too deep into the doctrine of salvation, we know that for all who respond to the calling of God, all things will work together for good because of the "justification", which happens at the point of salvation, and the "glorification", which is a lifetime process until we finish our journey on earth.

*Romans 8:28 **And WE KNOW that for those who love God, ALL THINGS WORK TOGETHER FOR GOOD, FOR THOSE WHO ARE CALLED ACCORDING TO HIS PURPOSE. FOR THOSE WHOM HE FOREKNEW (LOVED) HE ALSO PREDESTINED TO BE CONFORMED TO THE IMAGE OF HIS SON, in order that He might be the firstborn among many***

brothers. And those whom He PREDESTINED He also CALLED, and those whom He called He also JUSTIFIED, and those whom He justified He also GLORIFIED.

At this time, I would like to invite all who have not known Christ to make a decision to receive Christ-created faith and His favour or His grace so that you will return to His family as His son or daughter and receive all His goodness and you will start your journey of transformation to be the person God wants you to become – full of His glory.

Signs of Believers in Christ

The grace (undeserved favour) of God offered to mankind is a two-sided favour. On one side, the grace of God forgives all of the sins of all men (and women) – in the past, in the present, and in the future. One of the terms of the New Covenant described in *Hebrews 8:12 (which was prophesied in Jeremiah 31:34)* says, **"For I will be merciful toward their iniquities, and I will remember their sins no more."** Can you imagine that God not only forgives our sins, but He does not remember our sins anymore – even the sin that you just committed five minutes ago? Amazing! Why? Look at the next verses, **"And because of Him you are in Christ Jesus, who became to us wisdom from God; righteousness and sanctification and redemption, so that, as it is written, "Let the one who boasts, boast in the Lord."** (*1 Corinthians 1:30-31*) The moment you believe and decide to accept the faith and the grace, which is personified in Jesus Christ Himself, Jesus has become the *"wisdom of God"*. What is the wisdom of God, which is often referred to as foolishness by many people, especially the wise people of the world? Though the wisdom of God is very broad, it centers on the *"righteousness, the sanctification and the redemption"* through Christ. What are those terms?" When we are *"justified"*, we have been declared *"not guilty"* or *"righteous"* in the legal court of God. When we are *"sanctified"*, we have been separated from the world, and we now belong to God and are called for His purpose. Just like the *"holy"* items used in the Tabernacle of Moses or the Temple of Solomon, we have been separated and made worthy to be used as instruments of worship to God. When we are *"redeemed"*, our debts have been paid. We were slaves of sin, but we have been *"purchased"* by Jesus Christ using His blood as *"ransom"*. This means we have been "liberated" from the slavery of sin and its bondages. We have also been freed from the punishment for our sins and the curses for breaking the law (the Torah). We are free indeed and now belong to Christ.

How about the other side of the grace of God? Many Christians focus only on the forgiveness of sin and on being spared from punishment in hell sometime in the future. How about the current life on Earth? Are we just living aimlessly, waiting for the time we die and go to heaven? No! The other side of the grace of

God pertains to the *"restoration"*. Restoration is often associated with bringing back a broken item to its original form, or at least very close to its original form. We are restored not only to the condition of Adam, or slightly lower than the condition of Adam, we have been restored to a higher or better level than the original. When Adam fell to sin, it took God years to plan and deliver redemption. As a New Creation, God remembers our sins no more. What? Yes, it is true! *Hebrews 8:12* says, ***"For I will be merciful to their unrighteousness, and their sins and their lawless deeds I will remember no more."*** This Scripture should give us assurance and confidence that we are "forever" saved. It should take away any fear in us – fear of abandonment, fear of punishment, and fear of not having enough.

Let me make a list of some of the restorations that we are experiencing as a New Covenant believer:

- Restoration of our Relationship with God to Live in the Perfect Love of God,

- Restoration of our Position as the People of God in His Kingdom,

- Restoration to be the Sons and Daughters of God,

- Restoration to be His beloved, the Bride of Christ,

- Restoration of the Dominion and the Authority of God,

- Restoration of the Wisdom of God and the Power of God,

- Restoration of All Blessings,

- Restoration of Inheritance as Sons and Daughters of the Father,

- Restoration of Ownership as the Bride of Christ,

- Restoration of the Glory of God within Us,

- Restoration of God's Purpose and Calling in our lives,

- Restoration to Walk According to this Calling.

Before Jesus assigned His disciples to the Great Commission to go into the world and preach the gospel to every creature, he reminded them of the power of God and the wisdom of God that had been imparted to them. Jesus would not send them unless He had equipped them with the necessary tools. His word is not only for the first-century believers but also for us. We are intended to experience the same wisdom and power of God described in the Book of Acts. Take a look at the word of Jesus in *Mark 16:15-18, **"And He said to them, "Go into all the world and preach the gospel to every creature. He who believes and is baptized will be saved, but he who does not believe will be condemned. And these signs will follow*** *those who believe: IN MY NAME THEY WILL CAST OUT DEMONS; THEY WILL SPEAK WITH NEW TONGUES; THEY WILL TAKE UP SERPENTS; AND IF THEY DRINK ANYTHING DEADLY, IT WILL BY NO MEANS HURT THEM; THEY WILL LAY HANDS ON THE SICK, AND THEY WILL RECOVER."* These are the signs of the people who believe in Jesus Christ. I hope you all believe that these signs will accompany you in your life: your family, your ministry, your work, and your relaxing time.

Greater Works Than Jesus

The signs of believers in Christ described by Jesus were amazingly powerful. They point to the glory of Jesus' wisdom and power that attracted people to come to Him, and also to His disciples in the first-century church. Further to that, Jesus told His disciples a more amazing statement regarding people who believe in Him. This is His own word; thus, there is no reason for us to doubt His word. I would like you all to pay attention and sit tight because His statement will blow your mind.

Most assuredly, I say to you, he who believes in Me, THE WORKS THAT I DO HE WILL DO ALSO; and GREATER WORKS THAN THESE HE WILL DO, because I go to My Father, and whatever you ask in My name, that I will do, that the Father may be glorified in the Son. If you ask anything in My

name, I will do it. … and I will pray the Father, and He will give you another HELPER, that He may abide with you forever—the SPIRIT OF TRUTH… *(John 14:12-17)*

He started with *"most assuredly"!* In other words, He said, "Pay attention because it is a powerful word of truth. It means He guaranteed this promise. This is an air-tight promise by the Son of God, who will never lie nor change. Not only will we do the same things that He did, we will do greater things that Jesus did while He was on earth. What did Jesus do? He performed *"signs, wonders, and miracles"*. Signs are about the fulfillment of things that have been foretold or prophesied and sometimes refer to the occurrences in nature, especially in the sky. Wonders are about the manifestation of the power of God and are often related to God's works with nature. A miracle is often also called *"power" (Gk.dynamis)*. The working of miracles is one of the gifts of the Holy Spirit – available to all believers. Jesus fulfilled all prophecies concerning Himself written in the Old Testament. Jesus calmed the storm and even walked on the stormy water. Jesus turned water into wine and multiplied five loaves of bread and two fish to feed five thousand men, plus women and children. Jesus caused the disciples to catch abundant fish – twice. He made coins to pay taxes for himself, and Peter came out of the mouth of a fish. Everyone who came to Him for healing received their healing, and He resurrected several people from death. The word of God declares that greater works than these we, the believers in Christ, will do. I have seen, at least in reports or videos, many miracles happening in some countries far away, but only a few in the modern society of the developed countries. Am I missing something? Did Jesus imply there are *"greater works"* we do not know of?

In *John 6:38-40,* Jesus said, ***"For I have come down from heaven, not to do my own will but the will of him who sent me. And this is the will of him who sent me, that I should lose nothing of all that he has given me, but raise it up on the last day. For this is the will of my Father, that everyone who looks on the Son and believes in him should have eternal life, and I will raise him up on the last day."*** **The miracles Jesus did were important, but they were just a means to achieve the ultimate goal – that everybody is saved and will have eternal life. Eternal life is the** *"intimate knowing of the Father and of Jesus Christ".* Now I can see that we, the church, have done a decent job of bringing many people to know Christ and the Father. However, the majority of people have not known Jesus and the Father yet. Yes, I believe we, the believers in Christ, will do wonders and miracles, but the greatest wonder and miracle of all is the salvation of the people.

DEDO SUWANDA

CHAPTER 3

THE TRANSFORMATION PROCESS, SUFFERINGS AND DISCIPLINE

The Journey to Glory Has Started

Ever since the prophecy of Isaiah 60 became a revelation in my heart, I committed myself to pursue this. This is a promise from God, and I desire all His promises to be fulfilled in my life. I inquired God often how can the glory of the Lord be manifested in me because I have not seen such promise – not even a glimpse – manifesting in my life. He answered my prayer. When I was preparing for a Bible Study on the *Book of Romans*, which Martin Luther called the *"purest Gospel of Jesus Christ"*, God led me to this verse in chapter 8, which I considered the pinnacle of the Book of Romans.

Romans 8:30 **And those whom he predestined He also called, and those whom He called He also justified, and those whom He justified He also glorified.**

This verse gave me new hope. I know I have been justified. I belong to the group of people that have been *"predestined, called, and justified"*. Therefore, I will be glorified! Note this invitation was offered to all people. This verse got me excited. As a person with an engineering background – full of a critical and logical mind – I decided to pursue this promise in a "systematic way". Yes, I am accustomed to flowcharts and process diagrams. I believe God knows me well, with all my methods and way of thinking. Sure enough, God led me to another *"key"* verse.

2 Corinthians 3:18 (ESV) **And we all, with unveiled face, beholding the glory of the Lord, are being transformed into the same image from one degree of glory to another. For this comes from the Lord who is the Spirit.**

2 Corinthians 3:18 (NKJV) **But we all, with unveiled face, beholding as in a mirror the glory of the Lord, are being transformed into the same image from glory to glory, just as by the Spirit of the Lord.**

There is a valid reason why I use the same verse in two different translations. If you notice, the minor difference is the word *"as in a mirror"*. If you can be patient, you will see the significance later. However, at this time I would like to break down this "key" verse piece by piece because you will see the logical steps in the process of transformation into the glory of Jesus Christ.

The Veil Blinds the Minds and the Hearts

With my sincere heart's desire, I really want to be transformed into the image of Christ, with all the glory that He has. I can see a pattern of transformation, and I commit myself to figuring out the process. The verse starts with *"we all, with unveiled face"*. What does this mean? What does a veil have anything to do with the process? The good thing was that God had prepared me for this. I learned the principle *"let the Bible explain the Bible"*, which means we can always find an explanation of something that is "unclear" in another verse in the Bible – often just a few verses before or after. Let us see a few verses before,

But their minds were blinded. For until this day, the same veil remains unlifted in the reading of the Old Testament, because the veil is taken away in Christ. But even to this day, when Moses is read, a veil lies on their heart. Nevertheless, when one turns to the Lord, the veil is taken away. *(2 Corinthians 3:14-16)*

The same word, "veil," was mentioned four times in verses 14 to 16. This word must have a significant meaning. A veil is a thin fabric that is used to cover a face. A bride covers her face with a veil before meeting her groom at the altar. Moses covered his face with a veil when he came down from Mount Sinai. His face shone brilliantly with the glory of God after meeting God on the mountain, but the glory was fading away. He covered his face with a veil because he did not want the Israelites to see the fading glory on his face. Regardless of the purpose, a veil will always hinder the view of the users. The thicker the veil, the harder it is to see through.

The apostle Paul explained how the minds and the hearts of the Israelites in the Old Testament were *"blinded by a veil"* every time they read the Old Testament, especially the *"Moses"*, which are the first five books of the Old Testament. Also, the term *"Moses"* refers to the *"Law of Moses"* or *"Torah"*. The verse also explained that this veil could be taken away in Christ – the New Testament's *"Gospel of Grace"*. The apostle Paul went further in verse 15, saying that *"even to this day when Moses is read"* a veil lies in their *heart"*. Does it mean that my heart is blinded when I read the Law?

St. Augustine said, *"The Old is in the New Revealed; the New is in the Old Concealed"*. What does it mean? The Old Testament and the New Testament are related closely. They are not separate, but they are linked. The Old Testament is all about Jesus. On the day of Resurrection, Jesus appeared to His disciples who were in hiding and explained to them the plan of the purpose of God based on what was written in the Old Testament. Everything written in the Old Testament, including all prophecies and the Law of Moses, is about Jesus.

"These are MY WORDS that I spoke to you while I was still with you, that everything written about me in the LAW OF MOSES and THE PROPHETS and THE PSALMS must be fulfilled." THEN HE OPENED THEIR MINDS TO UNDERSTAND THE SCRIPTURES, and said to them, "Thus IT IS WRITTEN, that the Christ should suffer and on the third day rise from the dead, and that repentance for the forgiveness of sins should be proclaimed in his name to all nations, beginning from Jerusalem." (Luke 24:44-47)

It is imperative that we read the Old Testament, including the Law of Moses, with Jesus Christ in perspective. He is the only one who can lift the veil so that we can see "clearly" – whether we read the Old Testament or even the New Testament. Everything written in the Bible is about Jesus: who He is, who we are in Him, what He did at the cross, and all the benefits that have been given to us.

Beholding as in a Mirror the Glory of the Lord

This is an important step in the process of transformation into the image of Christ. How do we behold or look at the glory of Christ, our Lord, as in a mirror? Before we dive deeper into this step, let us dive into the story of the Bronze Serpent in the *21ˢᵗ chapter of the Book of Numbers*. The Book of Numbers depicts a low level point of the Israelites in the journey through the wilderness. Thirty-eight years after leaving Egypt, accompanied by great promises of God and followed by amazing signs and wonders, they were no further ahead than at the beginning. All the adults leaving Egypt, except Moses, Joshua, and Caleb, had died in the wilderness because of disobedience. They failed to arrive at the Promised Land – a place of *"rest"* God planned for them – *"the large and beautiful cities they did not build, the houses full of all good things they did not fill, the hewn-out wells they did not dig, and the vineyards and the olive trees they did not plant, but they filled them well."*

Many Christians are in similar circumstances as the so-called "Moses Generation" – born again, baptized, and even filled with the Holy Spirit, but have not entered the "rest" *(Hebrews 4)* and still rely on their own ability to survive daily lives. They are wandering in the wilderness of worldly life – just like the regular worldly people around them. There is almost no glory seen in their lives – nothing can be seen by people to attract them to come. Like the Israelites, the Moses-Generation Christians complained and were angry and displeased with God and His appointed leaders. They dream, talk, pray, and hope they would arrive at the rest, but they went around and around for years in the same place. They pray for revivals and visitation of the glory of God. Like Moses, they see the Promised Land, but they cannot enter and possess the Promised Land. What's wrong?

The Israelites were warned by God in the *Book of Numbers* because God was expressing His mercy and loving kindness to them. They were reminded of the hope and promise of the life God intended for them. God allowed *"fiery serpents"*, any negative consequences of sin, such as sicknesses, depression, oppression, striving, conflicts, despair, etc., among the people, and they bit the people, and many of the people of Israel died. They came to Moses and cried out, **"We have sinned, for we have spoken against the Lord and against you; pray to the Lord that He take away the serpents from us."** *(Numbers 21:7).* So Moses prayed for the people. Then the Lord said to Moses, **"Make a fiery serpent, and set it on a pole; and it shall be that everyone who is bitten when he looks at it, shall live."** *(Numbers 21:8)* So Moses made a bronze serpent, and put it on a pole; so it was if a serpent had bitten anyone when he looked at the bronze serpent, he lived.

The Bronze serpent on the pole is a picture of Jesus on the cross. The New Testament explained, **"And as Moses lifted up the serpent in the wilderness, even so must the Son of Man be lifted up, that whoever believes in Him should not perish but have eternal life.** *(John 3:14-15)* When we look at Jesus at the cross and believe what He has done for us, we receive salvation for our spirit and soul.

Let us look at the Amplified version of the Bible**, "And Moses made a serpent of bronze and put it on a pole, and if a serpent had bitten any man when he looked to the serpent of bronze [ATTENTIVELY, EXPECTANTLY, WITH A STEADY AND**

ABSORBING GAZE], he lived. (Numbers 21:9 (AMPC). We are supposed to look and observe Jesus at the cross attentively, expectantly, steadily, and with an absorbing gaze. You will be drawn to what you look at attentively, expectantly, and steadily and start to absorb what you see. Some people said that the Niagara Falls caused people to commit suicide. The fact is that when a person sees a gigantic amount of water pouring for 100 meters, continually, he may be drawn into the flow of water. Whatever you look long enough, you will dive into it.

How do you behold or look at the glory of Christ? The whole Bible, both the Old Testament and the New Testament, is about Jesus Christ – who He is, why He came to the earth, what He has accomplished, and the benefits we have received. He fully accomplished what the Fathers assigned Him to do, and He was glorified because of that. You will see His glory everywhere in the Bible. Jesus told the Pharisees, *"For if you believed Moses (The Law), you would believe Me; for he wrote about Me. But if you do not believe his writings, how will you believe My words?" (John 5:46)* After His resurrection, Jesus told His disciples who were hiding due to fear, *"These are the words which I spoke to you while I was still with you, that all things must be fulfilled which were written in the Law of Moses and the Prophets and the Psalms concerning Me." (Luke 24:44)* Everything that is written in the Old Testament is about Jesus Christ with all His glory. The apostle Paul wrote, ***"He (Jesus) is the image of the invisible God, the firstborn over all creation.*** *(Colossians 1:15)* You are able to find and see the glory of Christ everywhere in the Bible. The more you read the Bible, under the guidance of the Holy Spirit, you will see the glory of Christ more and more.

You will also see the glory of Christ in your daily experience with Him. He walks with you, speaks to you, heals you, saves you from troubles, meets your needs, comforts you, elevates you, and eventually glorifies you. All the goodness of God directed towards you shows the glory of God, but unfortunately, many Christians are not sensitive enough to recognize and see His glory in their lives. The more you recognize and are aware of His glory around you, the more you behold it. Therefore, behold the glory of Jesus ATTENTIVELY, EXPECTANTLY, WITH A STEADY AND ABSORBING GAZE, and do it as you see in the mirror. Whatever you see is also your reflection, thus the glory of Jesus will be absorbed into yourself.

Being Transformed into The Same Image from One Degree of Glory to Another

As you behold the glory of Christ, even as in the mirror, which means you are identifying His glory to yourself, you will be transformed into the image of Christ. We are made to conform to be like Christ. The Father, who is not bound by time or space, has seen us transformed. It is written in 1 John 4:17 ***"Love has been perfected among us in this: that we may have boldness in the day of judgment; because as He is, so are we in this world."*** God, who is love, has perfected us. We, who are still in this world, are copycats of Jesus, who are in heaven.

In the Bible, we sometimes read that Jesus Christ is in us through the Holy Spirit. However, we also often read that we are in Christ. This is a more important truth. Having Jesus Christ in us is like drinking a glass of water. When we are in Christ, we are becoming one with Christ. A dollar note inside a wallet will travel to all places the wallet is going – to the drawer in the living room, to the pocket of a jeans, to the supermarket, or the movie theatre. Not only that, the dollar will not be visible to anybody as long it remains in the wallet. Similarly, when we are in Christ, God the Father sees us as Christ. His identity is our identity. His glory is our glory.

Let us examine what would be the identity of someone who is in Christ:

He is a NEW CREATION (2 Corinthians 5:17)

He has been RECONCILED and become a FRIEND OF GOD (2 Corinthians 5:19)

He is established in the LOVE and the GRACE OF GOD (1 Corinthians 1:4 & Romans 8:38)

He has been JUSTIFIED or made RIGHTEOUS,

He has been SANCTIFICIED or made HOLY,

He has been REDEEMED or PURCHASED by the blood of Jesus (1 Corinthians 1:30, 2 Corinthians 5:21)

He has been given the gift of NO CONDEMNATION (Romans 8:1)

He has been given ETERNAL LIFE (Romans 6:23)

He has been made SONS AND DAUGHTERS (Galatians 3:26)

He has a LIFE IN THE SPIRIT (Romans 8:10)

He has been BLESSED WITH ALL SPIRITUAL (PNEUMATIKOS) BLESSINGS (Ephesians 1:3)

His CURSE has been REPLACED BY BLESSINGS (Galatians 3: 13)

He can be an IMITATOR OF JESUS (1 Thessalonians 2:14)

He has been given the BLESSING OF ABRAHAM to be the HEIR OF THE WORLD (Galatians 3:14)

He has been made JOINT-HEIR WITH JESUS (Ephesians 1:11)

He has been made MORE THAN A CONQUEROR (2 Corinthians 2:14)

He can REIGN IN LIFE (Romans 5:17)

He has the ability to live a GODLY LIFE (2 Timothy 3:12)

He will KNOW THE WILL OF GOD (1 Thessalonians 5:18)

He has been ESTABLISHED AND ANOINTED FOR A CALLING (2 Corinthians 1:21)

He is ENCOURAGED TO GOOD WORKS (2 Thessalonians 3:12)

He can have the FULLNESS OF GOD (Colossians 2:9)

He can have an ETERNAL GLORY (1 Peter 5:10)

Wow! That's our identity in Christ! But why have I not seen it yet? Why have my neighbours not seen such glory in me? As *2 Corinthians 3:18* indicates, the process of transformation will be from one level of glory to another. It is a step-by-step process, and it may take some time. In fact, it is a lifetime journey. It is our journey to glory – the "process of glorification". The good news is that we have several people who have walked ahead of us, including the apostle Paul. His teaching has been documented for our benefit. We understand that we determine the speed of transformation. It depends on how attentive, expectant, steady, and intense we absorb when we behold the glory of the Lord. As long as we gaze on Jesus at the cross – His glorious works – we will be transformed into His image from one level of glory to another.

Unfortunately, men are impatient, especially in the 21st century society. The word "instant" is attached to almost everything – instant camera, instant cereal, instant noodles, instant cash withdrawal, and many more. In 1965, Gordon Moore suggested computational progress would become significantly faster, smaller, and more efficient over time. Moore's Law estimated that computing capabilities will double every two years. Exponential growth is at the heart of the rapid increase of computing capabilities in the past 60 years. Assuming Moore's Law is still valid, the computing capabilities are 1 billion times that in 1965. People, especially the youth, are so accustomed to and spoiled by everything "instant". They may not have the patience in their journey to glory, but God's way always wins.

Just as by The Spirit of The Lord

The apostle Paul gave the last clue of the transformation process. The Spirit of God is in charge of the transformation process. In the ESV translation, it says, *"For this comes from the Lord who is the Spirit."* In Christian circles, We are often told to be *"led by the Spirit"* or to *"walk by the Spirit"*. In Galatians 5:16-18, the Apostle Paul tells us, ***"So I say, walk by the Spirit, and you will not gratify the desires of the flesh. For the flesh desires what is***

contrary to the Spirit, and the Spirit what is contrary to the flesh. They are in conflict with each other, so that you are not to do whatever you want. But if you are led by the Spirit, you are not under the law."

There are several important points here. First, there is only one way to walk by the Spirit or to be led by the Spirit: you cannot be under the law. What does it mean? Aren't we a New Covenant believer under the grace of God? Yes, it is true. However, we have the tendency to drift back to the Law. Under the Gospel of Grace, all the required works have been done by Jesus – completely. It means *"Jesus alone is enough"*. We should not add anything else to be accepted by God, to be loved by God, or to receive blessings from God. How many Christians think, *"Only if I give more money or more time for the ministry in the church, then God will love me more and bless me more."* Many Christians also think that *"fasting will make God give you what you asked in prayer"*. They think that you need to "do more" to be loved by God more, or the blessings from God depend on the additional requirements, such as fasting and charity work. This is like "bribing" God to get something you want. They think that the finished work of Christ is not enough, and you must do something to make it more perfect. Jesus said at the cross, *"It is finished"*. Nothing can be added.

Second, if you walk by the Spirit, you will not follow the desires of the flesh. The flesh is your own desires and will. What happens if you are following the desires of your flesh? *Galatian 5:19-21* clearly describes the *"work of the flesh"*: *"adultery, fornication, uncleanness, lewdness, idolatry, sorcery, hatred, contentions, jealousies, outbursts of wrath, selfish ambitions, dissensions, heresies, envy, murders, drunkenness, revelries, and the like."* They are very unattractive. The opposites are the fruit of the Spirit: *"love, joy, peace, longsuffering, kindness, goodness, faithfulness, gentleness, self-control"* (Galatians 5:22-23). The fruit of the Spirit is the characteristics of Jesus Christ – the glory of Christ. Thus, the apostle Paul is clear that trying to perform the requirement of the law will lead you to the *"work of the flesh"*.

Let me repeat the first point. How can you walk by the Spirit or be led by the Spirit? The apostle Paul is very clear with the truth. At the end of *Galatians 5:18,* he said, *"But if you are led by the Spirit, you are not under the law."* Then he reemphasized it in *Galatians 5:23, "Against such (fruit of the Spirit) there is no law."* He also declared in *1 Corinthians 15:56, "The sting of death is sin, and the strength of sin is the law."* New Testament believers are supposed to be free from the law because Jesus Christ had fulfilled the law for us. The law still exists because Jesus did not abolish it, but he fulfilled it so that we don't have to. We now live in the Spirit of life and are led by the Spirit so that we can go through the process of transformation smoothly.

The Holy Spirit is our Helper *(Gk. parakletos)*. He will teach us all things and guide us into all truth *(John 16:13)*. He will bring us to the remembrance of all things that Jesus said (and did). He will bear witness about Jesus. *(John 15:26)*. He will declare to us the things that are to come *(John 16:13)*. He imparts wisdom and revelation to the believers and illuminate their hearts so that they understand the plan and purpose of God *(Ephesians 1:15)*. He equips us spiritual gifts (power of God) for our ministry *(1 Corinthians 12:1)*. He produces the fruit of the Spirit into our lives, and sets us apart or sanctifies us *(Galatian 5:22)*. He intercedes for us in times of weaknesses according to the perfect will of the Father *(Romans 8:26)*. He is our Comforter, especially during our time of trouble and weakness. *(John 14:16)*. We, the believers in Christ, will go through the process of transformation into the image of Christ with the help of the Holy Spirit. The word "helper" is not meant to be someone at a lower rank or power, but it means the empowerment and the supplier of all abilities to succeed. Without the Holy Spirit, it is impossible for anyone to go through the process.

From Suffering to Glory

I enjoy watching movies especially about "underdogs" emerging as winners. In Rocky IV, after reclaiming the boxing championship title, Rocky Balboa (Sylvester Stallone) plans to retire and live a quiet life with his wife, Adrian. However, during an exhibition match, Rocky's friend Apollo Creed was mercilessly beaten to death by a strong and feisty Russian rookie, Ivan Drago. Rocky challenged Ivan to a Christmas Day fight. He knew how strong Ivan was, and despite his age, he committed to training for this seemingly impossible fight. He trained intensely above and beyond the training he had in his past life. There were times when he almost gave up, and despite the opinions of people around him, he continued his goal to defeat the "giant" in front of him. In the end, with his swelling and bloodied face, Rocky lifted up his hands in a glorious victory. What a scene that millions of people who watched the movie still remember decades later.

God has promised us that His glory will be seen in the believers. However, the apostle Paul also warned us that the journey to glory would be full of pain and suffering. ***"The Spirit Himself bears witness with our spirit that we are children of God, and if children, then heirs—heirs of God and joint heirs with Christ, if indeed we suffer with Him, that we may also be glorified together. For I consider that the sufferings of this present time are not worthy to be compared with the glory which shall be revealed in us."*** *(Romans 8:16-18)* However, he encouraged us all that the sufferings that we would experience, together with Christ, were unworthy compared to the glory that would be revealed in us. The glory will be extraordinary that *"the whole creation is eagerly waiting of the revealing of the glory of the sons of God"*. We are living in this *"hope", the "hope of glory"*. We were saved in this hope, but hope is something that will happen in the future, though it is guaranteed by the *"forever faithful"* God. Therefore, he urged us to *"eagerly wait for it with perseverance"*.

Perseverance is a word often used to encourage people to keep on going despite severe challenges. I sense that the word is often lightly used. Let us see how we can persevere in life. The apostle Paul also wrote in *Romans 5:1-5,* ***"Not only that, but we rejoice in our sufferings, knowing that suffering produces endurance, and endurance produces character, and character produces hope, and hope does not put us to shame, because God's love has been poured into our hearts through the Holy Spirit who has been given to us."*** The apostle Paul instructed us to "rejoice" in our sufferings because this is the only path to *"endurance" (ESV)* or *"perseverance" (NKJV).* No wonder many people, even long-time Christians, cannot persevere when trials and tribulations come their way. Note that God does not create suffering, but Satan or the Devil is the creator of tribulations and suffering. They may come to us directly or indirectly through the people around us and often through the people we love and who are supposed to love us. We also find ourselves in trials or tribulations due to our own mistakes. Regardless of the source of the problems, God often allows them to happen because God will use them for our own benefit. We love this verse, ***"And we know that for those who love God, all things work*** *together for good, for those who are called according to his purpose." (Romans 8:28).* God always turns lemons into lemonade for those who are called for His purpose. We all have been predestined to such a calling; thus, suffering is a sure thing for us. Why? Because He loves us. God wants us to become the sons and daughters with His glory. Notice that *"endurance"* or *"perseverance"* will surely produce *"characters"* – the *"characters of God"* or the *"glory of God"*.

There are times when it seems that the trials and tribulations are unbearable. However, we know that God is faithful and will not let you be tried beyond your strength, but with every trial and tribulation, He will surely provide a way out that you may be able to bear. The Bible teaches us that *"the Spirit also helps in our weaknesses."* During the lowest and the darkest time of my life, when my strength was at the lowest when I ran out of ideas on how to get out of the pit, and when we do not even know what to ask from God except to take me out of this deep and dark pit, I remember the words of God, ***"For we do not know what we should pray for as we ought, but the Spirit Himself makes intercession for us with groanings which cannot be uttered. Now He who searches the hearts knows what the mind of the Spirit is because He makes intercession for the saints according to the will of God."*** *(Romans 8:26-27)* The Spirit of God will intercede of and pray the most perfect prayer, which is according to the perfect will of God. This prayer is often in the form of groanings that cannot be uttered or described with words. It may sound strange, but I found salvation from a dark situation that I cannot imagine I can get out of.

Breaking the Outer Man

God intended for us to walk in the Holy Spirit and to be led by the Holy Spirit because He is the Spirit of truth, faith, love, life, revelation, wisdom, power, holiness, gentleness, and many of God's glory. When we were born again, God made our spirit alive and inseparable from the Holy Spirit. The question is why our lives are not reflecting the glory of God – most of the time. We need to understand what constitutes a "man" or, in a politically correct term, a "person". According to the doctrine of "Trichotomy", a man consists of the spirit, the soul, and the body.

Our spirit is our "Inner Man"; it becomes alive and becomes one with the Holy Spirit at the time of born again experience. The term "alive" simply means in the presence of communion with God, and "death" means separation from God. Our soul is our "Outer Man" and consists of our mind, emotions, and will. We think with our mind and feel with our emotions. Either our mind or our emotions will instruct our will to make a decision to do something. Most people, especially unbelievers whose spirits are dead, make contact with other people either intellectually or emotionally using their mind and their emotions. Our body is just a shell that will grow old and die eventually, and it will be replaced by a "glorious" body – the same body that Jesus got after His resurrection.

A Spirit-led man is supposed to live led by the Holy Spirit. This is only possible when his spirit, together with the Holy Spirit, is in control of himself. Since a born-again man has a God-given "free will", he can decide whether he wants to be controlled by his spirit or by his soul. Note that the soul is often referred to as "flesh" or "self", which causes a man to sin. Unfortunately, most men live under the control of their flesh, especially when the law is in the mix. *"For when we were in the flesh, the sinful passions which were aroused by the law were at work in our members to bear fruit to death."* (Romans 7:5)

Watchman Nee wrote in his book "Breaking the Outer Man", that unless the Outer Man is "broken" or "tamed", our Inner Man cannot be released and lead a Spirit-led life. An "unbroken" horse is useless for a soldier in a war, regardless of how strong or fast that horse is. An "unbroken" man without restraint from God cannot be used by God for His purpose regardless of his strength, his sharp mind, or his wealth. The "living water" cannot flow out of our belly freely. God intended us to be sanctified, glorified, and perfected, but we have to go through the transformation process, which is the work of the Holy Spirit throughout our lives. The Spirit is to break and dismantle our Outer Man so that our Inner Man can flow out and shine. This is what the apostle Paul refers to as *"die to self"* or *"discipline process"*. When we were born again, we *"died to sin"* together with Christ. Then, we should go through the process of *"die to the law"*, *"die to self"*, and finally, *"die to our own ability"* – so that we can live a life fully trusting and dependent on God. This is the life that God called us into - from before we were created. Our resistance to the breaking or the dying process will only delay the process of transformation.

Here are some characteristics of people whose "Outer Man" has been broken:

➢ Abiding in the presence of God more constantly, regardless of activities and busyness,

➢ Ability to tap into the mind of Christ and think like Christ,

- Ability to have the emotion of Christ and to have His compassion,

- Ability to have the perfect will of the Father and to make decisions accordingly,

- Ability to receive the Spirit of Revelation and Understanding, and be inspired by God's idea,

- Ability to Hear God more frequently and accurately,

- Ability to Deliver the Word of God from our spirit, as the Spirit leads,

- Godly characters are reflected more in their lives,

- Ability to operate more with the wisdom and power of God,

- More powerful testimonies from their lives,

- Ability to touch other people's spirit with our spirit and vice versa,

- Ability to measure or discern others - beyond their mind and emotion,

- The glory of God will be seen in them, even by unbelievers.

I Will Finish the Race

There is another term used in the Bible to describe this process – the discipline process. God reminded us in *Hebrews 12:5-6:*

"My son, do not regard lightly the discipline of the Lord, nor be weary when reproved by him. For the Lord disciplines the one he loves and chastises every son whom he receives."

The Scripture further explains, *"It is for discipline that you have to endure. God is treating you as sons. For what son is there whom his father does not discipline? If you are left without discipline, in which all have participated, then you are illegitimate children and not sons."* *(Hebrews 12:7-8)* God disciplines us for our good so that we may share His holiness and His glory. The Scripture finally instructed us, *"Therefore lift your drooping hands and strengthen your weak knees, and make straight paths for your feet."* *(Hebrews 12:12-13)* We are told to continue our daily walk – our journey to glory. This is the race that the apostle Paul instructed us to participate in. He said, *"Do you not know that in a race, all the runners run, but only one receives the prize? So run that you may obtain it."* *(1 Corinthians 9:24).* Ever since I became a believer in Christ in 1999, I have been on this journey – the marathon race of a Christian life. I am praying and believing that I, one day soon, will say what the apostle Paul said in his old age, *"I have fought the good fight, I have finished the race, I have kept the faith."* (2

Timothy 4:7) I will fight the good fight. I will keep the faith that Jesus Christ gave me. And I will finish the race!

DEDO SUWANDA

CHAPTER 4

ENTERING THE TIME OF

ACCELERATION

I remember studying "Physics" and "Mechanics" during my high school and university period. I had to learn about distance, speed, and acceleration in relation to time. Speed or velocity is defined as the rate of change of distance, or in a simpler term, how much distance has been covered in a particular time. On the other hand, acceleration is defined as the rate of change of speed or velocity per unit of time. At a time of acceleration, everything moves faster with time, and the distance or the quantity increases exponentially.

One day, God gave me a mental picture of a bow and an arrow. The archer loaded the arrow at the bowstring and drew the arrow and the bowstring as far as possible. Then he released the bowstring, and I could see the arrow flew very fast. I am sensing that we are in a time period of maximum stretching, and the bowstring is about to be released. There is severe stress and strain during the stretching period, but we are experiencing acceleration and exponential growth now – in a spiritual realm.

I asked a question in Chapter 1, "What time is it now?" Before we answer that question, I would like to introduce you to a gifting and anointing with regard to God's timing. Jesus is the *"Anointed One"*. Since we are in Christ, we have also been given His anointing, including the anointing to know the time and seasons. It is often referred to as the "Issachar" anointing. Issachar is one of the twelve sons of Jacob. His clan has been anointed to know time and season and the wisdom to advise the kings on what to do with the information. We have been given the same anointing to know the timing of God; some have a stronger anointing than others. But we are all able to discern the time and season the church is in now and understand the wisdom of what to do in this season. I like to use the term *"divine knowing"*. God often put in my heart to *"know"* when and what is about to happen.

I know and believe we are the *"Benjamin Generation"* who live in the *"eleventh hour"*, or even *"five minutes before midnight"*. We do not know exactly when Jesus will return, but we know (without going too deep into the subject of End Time) that the time is near. We have seen prophetic signs and fulfilments as never before. We have discerned the period described in *Isaiah 60:2: "For behold, darkness shall cover the earth, and thick darkness the peoples"*. In addition, I am also sensing that the verse in *Isaiah 60:22b, "I am the LORD; in its time I will hasten it"* is in motion. We have entered the *"Time of Acceleration"*.

Acceleration in Technology and Finances

The acceleration of technological development in the 20th century could not be imagined by the people living in the early 1900's. The progress started with the development of steam engines, the discovery of crude oil, the development of internal combustion engines for transportation vehicles, the invention of electricity, the first DC and then followed the AC current, the invention of the computer, and the creation of silicon with subsequent circuit boards and microchips. In a parallel process, the information technology and the media technology triggered a faster acceleration of technology innovation. Travelling has become faster and more accessible, and with the increased efficiency and effectiveness of rocket engineering, people are aiming to go to Mars. However, the most recent acceleration in nanotechnology, artificial intelligence, and DNA/genetic modifications have made ethical scientists, engineers, and governmental leaders either ambitiously optimistic or filled with doomsday fear. Regardless of their point of view, it is undeniable that technological advancement seems to be out of control.

In the area of finance, the picture is very similar. A century ago, people around the world used coins and bills as money for trading. Governments must have enough gold to print money, thus securing money as a stable and reliable currency. In the late 19th century, central banks were formed in countries in Europe. Central banks are not owned or controlled by governments but by private bankers and well-off individuals. In the early 1900's, these European bankers managed to convince the congress in the USA, through deception and corruption, to establish the US central bank, the Federal Reserve Bank. It is owned by bankers and well-off private individuals – many are Europeans. It owns the power to create money without the security of gold. It lends money to the US government, banks, and governments around the world – with very limited oversight. Inflation went out of hand as a lot of money was printed without much constraint. The situation has worsened during the Covid-19 pandemic. It is estimated that more than 40% of the money in circulation in the USA was printed only in the past 3.5 years. In the past few years, digital currencies have been created. Crypto currencies were created by unknown parties.

Due to the limited amount of currencies issued, some Crypto currencies, such as Bitcoin and Ethereum, increased in value over time. It is good to a certain extent because it is a market-driven economy, but central banks and governments did not like it because it competes with their created currencies. Governments and bankers in many countries did not want to miss out on the opportunity, and created CBDC's (Central Bank Digital Currency). Driven by evil intentions, many countries use the CBDC as a way to control people's lives. These countries will eventually plan to eliminate cash based on a "noble reason" to eliminate "black market" trading. The European Union (EU) has passed the law that cash transactions over Euro 1,000 are considered law-breaking. Chinese governments can stop any payment transactions by people whom they disapprove of or dislike. I can see how the "difficult-to-understand" prophecy, such as *Revelation 13:17*, ***"so that no one can buy or sell unless he has the mark, that is, the name of the beast or the number of its name",*** is likely to be fulfilled in the near future.

Different sources have also confirmed in the past few years that genetically modified viruses, such as Covid-19, can be manufactured in laboratories. We also learned that mRNA vaccines can be produced in a much shorter time than traditional vaccines. Though unproven and its side-effects are still unknown, this technology shows acceleration in biotechnology and health science. The rampant use of GMO (genetically modified crops (and livestock) has also accelerated to the point of the danger of ruining the vegetation and the animals God created.

Acceleration in World Population

We have also seen the acceleration of the population growth in the world. Despite deaths due to sicknesses, wars, and poverty, the world population has grown exponentially. Refer to the chart below. According to the data from *"Our World in Data" (OurWorldinData.org)*, the world's population at the time of Jesus walking on earth was only 190 million. In the 14th century, a quarter of the world's population (including half of the population in Europe) died due to the Black Death pandemic, but the exponential growth continued. The population grew to almost a billion by 1800 and 1.65 billion by 1900. Despite the two World Wars in the 1900s, the population growth continued. Perhaps it was driven by the advances in technology and health. By 1999, the end of the second millennium, six billion people inhabited the earth. In less than a quarter of a century since the start of the third millennium, the population has grown to about eight billion. This is an exponential growth, an acceleration of the world population.

The size of the world population over the last 12,000 years

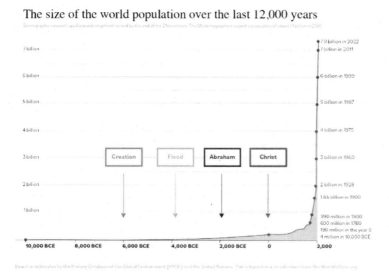

"Israel" Will Be Restored – The Acceleration of the Church

The prophet Amos prophesied in 760 BC of the New Testament Age. At that time, the Tabernacle of David, a tent built by King David to house the Ark of the Covenant where the presence of God resides, has been destroyed and has disappeared. Amos prophesied that the Tabernacle of David would be rebuilt to its former glory at the time of his reign. King David was the greatest king of the United Kingdom of Israel, under whom Israel was a united kingdom under one king.

"On that day I will raise up

The tabernacle of David, which has fallen down,

And repair its damages;

I will raise up its ruins,

And rebuild it as in the days of old" (Amos 9: 11)

This prophecy speaks of the "Future Israel", the church in the New Testament. The church is the Tabernacle of David where the presence of God is taking residence. The Holy Spirit is residing in each one of us, the living stones of the dwelling place of God. Amos continued:

"Behold, the days are coming," says the Lord,

"When the plowman shall overtake the reaper,

And the treader of grapes him who sows seed; (Amos 9:13)

The days are here now! Can you imagine when *"the plowman shall overtake the reaper"* or when *"the treader of grapes are him who sow seeds."?* How should we interpret these verses? People who plow the ground are overtaking the people who harvest, and people who press the grapes are sowing the seeds of the grapes at the same time. It means that by the time we plan something, it is done! This means acceleration of time and supernatural growth. We are entering this period when God's plan is fulfilled almost immediately. Get ready for such a moment! We will see a new and supernatural move of God that we have never seen before.

What kind of acceleration did Amos prophesy? Let us read the next verse.

> *"I will bring back the captives of My people Israel;*
>
> *They shall build the waste cities and inhabit them;*
>
> *They shall plant vineyards and drink wine from them;*
>
> *They shall also make gardens and eat fruit from them."*
>
> *(Amos 9:14)*

He is prophesying a restoration of "Israel", the people of God. The "natural Israel" has recently been restored in 1948, but the "spiritual Israel", the descendants of Abraham by faith, the church, have been born since the death and resurrection of Jesus Christ. Those who were lost and in captivity by the enemy, the Devil, have been brought back to the dwelling place of God, the church. We will be an acceleration of the growth of the church, which is about the Great Harvest. Jesus spoke about it when a multitude of people came to Him after witnessing the signs and wonders. Jesus told the disciples, *"The harvest is plentiful, but the laborers are few; therefore, pray earnestly to the Lord of the harvest to send out laborers into his harvest."* (Matthew 9:37-38) Jesus is also now telling us the same thing! The Great Harvest is here, but there are not enough workers. Jesus told His disciples before and is telling us now to pray earnestly to God, the Lord of Harvest, to send out the workers.

Let us see the growth of the church, as defined by Jesus Christ, measured by the number of believers since the first century. Please refer to the graph below. There was a great multiplication of believers in the first century. The Book of Acts recorded the activities and the growth of the church despite opposition from the Jewish leaders and from the Roman Empire. On the day of Pentecost, 3000 new believers were added after Peter shared the Gospel under the anointing of the Holy Spirit *(Acts 2:41)*. The next few verses give us the vital key to the growth of the church:

"And they continued steadfastly in the apostles' doctrine and fellowship, in the breaking of bread, and in prayers. Then fear came upon every soul, and many wonders and signs were done through the apostles. Now all who believed were together, and had all things in common, and sold their possessions and goods, and divided them among all, as anyone had need. So, continuing daily with one accord in the temple and breaking bread from house to house, they ate their food with gladness and simplicity of heart, praising God and having favor with all the people. And the Lord added to the church daily those who were being saved." (Acts 2:42-47)

Three centuries later, when the Roman Empire institution-alized the "religion" of Christianity, the growth slowed. The church entered a period called "The Falling Away" or the "Dark Ages". Religion and legalism practices led to the hindrance of the work of the Holy Spirit and finally led to corruption and the loss of the true Gospel – until the Reformation in the 1500s led by Martin Luther. At that time, only about 1% of the world's population was considered "born-again Christian", a definition by Jesus to describe "church". The Reformation restarted the exponential growth of Christianity, starting in Europe but spreading worldwide. The outpouring of the Holy Spirit at the Azusa Street Revival led by William J. Seymour in 1906 and the Charismatic Movement in the Catholic Church in the late 1960s to early 1970s led to similar movements in other Christian mainline denominations. It gave more fuel to the church's growth. It is estimated that "born-again" Christians made up about 11% of the world population by 2010 (or 31% if Catholics and Orthodox are included). We expect such exponential growth to continue in the years to come. I cannot comprehend that the majority of people will not know Christ and will be left behind to go through the End Time Great Tribulation. I do believe that a significant number of people, including the practicing Jews, will come to Christ during the period of the Great Tribulation, but as the prophecy in the Book of Revelation has told us, they will have to experience severe trials and tribulations beyond what I could imagine.

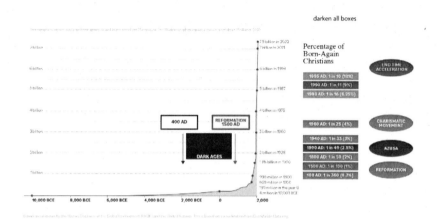

CHAPTER 5

THE NEW TESTAMENT WEALTH TRANSFER

Lift up your eyes all around, and see;

they all gather together, they come to you;

your sons shall come from afar,

and your daughters shall be carried on the hip.

Then you shall see and be radiant;

your heart shall thrill and exult,

because the abundance of the sea shall be turned to you,

the wealth of the nations shall come to you. (Isaiah 60:4:5)

The time is now! What is the urgency? What are we to do? We, the church, are instructed to "lift up our eyes all around and see". We are to be observant and to watch the mighty move of God. Remember the story of King Jehoshaphat in 2 Chronicles 20? The kingdom of Judah was attacked and surrounded by the enemy – the king of Ammon, Moab, and Mount Seir – who threatened to demolish him and the kingdom of Judah. Before God destroyed the enemy, God told him to "stand firm, hold your position, and see the salvation of the Lord on your behalf, O Judah and Jerusalem." In the same way, God wants us to witness His mighty power and His salvation from our enemy, the Devil. The warfare is spiritual. We are to defend all the victory, including the authority and power that Jesus gave us. We are already the light and the salt. His glory has been given to us, though it may be covered by our own "self". At the time of the Great Harvest, we will see the unsaved people gather together and come to us, the church because they will see "the light in us and the brightness of our rising" – the glory of the Lord in us. I can only imagine how easy it will be to do evangelism at this time. We do not have to do much, nor have to say much, but they will come when they see the glory of the Lord in us. This is not of our own doing but the great work of the Holy Spirit. The Holy Spirit will open the eyes of the hearts of many so that they will see the light of God and the glory of the Lord in the believers, and they will come.

Pay attention! The Scripture also says that "our hearts shall thrill and exult". There must be something more amazing coming our way. Not only will God cause the abundance of unbelievers in the church to increase, "nations" and their "kings" will bring "the abundance of the sea" to us. Note that the term "sea" in the Bible often refers to the "world". Thus, the "wealth of the world" or the "wealth of the nations" will be transferred to the church. This is a supernatural phenomenon. This is the wealth transfer that some Christians are foreseeing – "The Great Wealth Transfer". I highly recommend all to read Peter Youngren's book on this subject for reference.

Wealth Transfer in the Old Testament

Wealth Transfer from the people of the world ("the unrighteous") to the people of God ("the righteous") had happened before in the Old Testament - twice. The term "Wealth Transfer" may not be used to describe them, but the occurrences were truly supernatural acts of God to move wealth to the hands of God's chosen people for an intended purpose. God certainly intended to prosper His people as He promised from the very beginning, but there was a higher purpose for God prospering His people. It is to provide His people with resources? to build a dwelling place of God, the House of God, so that God can dwell among His people. God truly enjoys dwelling among His people, His beloved people. He takes pleasure to have fellowship with His beloved people, as a man would have the pleasure to be near his beloved wife, and children. Let us examine the two wealth transfers that happened in the Old Testament.

The First Wealth Transfer

Two thousand years after God created the world and its content, including the first man and woman, and after God started all over again with Noah and his family, God chose a man named Abraham and his wife Sarah to form God's chosen people. Abraham was deemed righteous not because of his deeds but because he believed in God and His promises. From Abraham, his son Isaac and his grandson Jacob (later called Israel), the nation of Israel formed. Jacob's eleventh but most beloved son, Joseph, was sold as a slave and sent to Egypt by his envious brothers. After the ups and downs of life in a foreign country, he became the second most powerful man in Egypt after Pharaoh. He saved the clan of Israel who would have otherwise perished due to a 7-year severe famine. For the next 400 years, the descendants of Jacob, Israel, grew into a large nation of at least 2 million people, but as slaves under severe oppression from Egypt.

After his failed self-effort to free the Israelites, and after hiding in the wilderness for 40 years, Moses, at the age of 80, was called by God to liberate the nation of Israel and to take them to the land that God promised Abraham to occupy – a land of milk and honey. Most importantly, God wanted to take them out of Egypt to serve Him, and God wanted to dwell among them. Eventually, God instructed them to build the Tabernacle, a transportable tent structure made of gold, silver, acacia wood, and other fine materials. It was His dwelling place among his chosen people. However, the Israelites had been slaves for over 400 years and had very little – without gold, silver, and other expensive materials. God is a "Covenant God" who is eager to prosper His people, especially in regard to building His dwelling place among His people. God always provided for the building of His house. He told Moses, who, in turn, told the congregation of Israel to ask the Egyptians for gold, silver, and other precious materials. He caused the Israelites to receive favour in the eyes of the Egyptians, who could not wait to see the Israelites leave their country after experiencing plague after plague, especially the tenth one, the death of the eldest males of the families and of the flocks.

And I will give this people favor in the sight of the Egyptians; and when you go, you shall not go empty, but each woman shall ask of her neighbor, and any woman who lives in her house, for silver and gold jewelry, and for clothing. You shall put them on your sons and on your daughters. So you shall plunder the Egyptians. ... The people of Israel had also done as Moses told them, for they had asked the Egyptians for silver and gold jewelry and for clothing. And the Lord had given the people favor in the sight of the Egyptians, so that they let them have what they asked. Thus, they plundered the Egyptians." (Exodus 3:21-36)

God's First Dwelling Place – The Tabernacle of Moses

The Israelites went through Passover, crossing the Red Sea on dry land and receiving the Ten Commandments and 603 other laws of the Torah. Knowing that not a single person, except Jesus Christ, is able to meet the strict requirements of the law, God instituted the Five Levitical Offerings as a way out of punishment for breaking the law. Herds of flocks must be killed on an altar as burnt offerings, peace offerings, or sin offerings. Subsequently, God instructed Moses to build a Tabernacle on earth, a duplicate of the Heavenly Tabernacle, its pattern shown by God to Moses. The Tabernacle of Moses was needed for the Israelites to perform offerings for the redemption of sins, but most importantly, it is the place where the presence of God dwelt – in the Most Holy Place. The gold, silver, and other precious materials plundered from the Egyptians were used to build the Tabernacle.

The Lord said to Moses, **"Speak to the people of Israel, that they take for me a contribution. … And this is the contribution that you shall receive from them: gold, silver, and bronze … And let them make me a sanctuary, that I may dwell in their midst. Exactly** *as I show you concerning the pattern of the tabernacle, and of all its furniture, so you shall make it." (Exodus 25:1-9)*

God's Second Dwelling Place – The Temple of Solomon

For almost 450 years, God dwelled among the Israelites in the Tabernacle of Moses. There was a period of time when the Israelites were not faithful to God; the Ark of the Covenant, which represented the presence of God, was taken away from them and was in the hands of the enemy, the Philistines. For a short period of time afterward, it was in the hands of a commoner. The Tabernacle of Moses became hollow because the presence of God was no longer there. David, known as "a man after God's own heart," desired to bring the Ark of the Covenant back to Jerusalem, the City of David. Once he brought it back, he built another Tabernacle, called the Tabernacle of David, to house the Ark of the Covenant. The nation of Israel prospered during the rule of David.

Many years later, the prosperous King David had a thought and desire. Let us examine what was written in 2 Samuel 7:1-13:

"King David was living in his palace, and the LORD had given him peace from all his enemies around him. Then David said to Nathan the prophet, "Look, I am living in a palace made of cedar wood, but the Ark of God is in a tent!" Nathan said to the king, "Go and do what you really want to do, because the LORD is with you." But that night the LORD spoke His word to Nathan,

"Go and tell My servant David, 'This is what the LORD says: Will you build a house for me to live in? From the time I brought the Israelites out of Egypt until now I have not lived in a house. I have been moving around all this time with a tent as My home. 7 As I have moved with the Israelites, I have never said to the tribes, ... "Why haven't you built Me a house of cedar?"' ... "'When you die and join your ancestors, I will make one of your sons the next king, and I will set up his kingdom. He will build a house for Me, and I will let his kingdom rule always."

Though King David desired to build a permanent and beautiful house for God, the Temple of God, God appointed his son, King Solomon, to build this temple. God gave David the design and the details of everything in the temple to David, who passed them on to Solomon. Not only that, King David contributed a significant amount of gold, silver, wood, and other precious materials for the construction of the temple.

God Provided the Finances Through David and His Household

The Tabernacle of Moses is a picture of the glory of God in the Old Testament, but the Temple of Solomon is much more glorious, and it is a picture of the glory of God in the New Testament. It is difficult to estimate the cost of the material and the labour to build the temple. Let us examine what the Bible recorded.

"And David the king said to all the assembly, "Solomon my son, whom alone God has chosen, is young and inexperienced, and the work is great, for the palace will not be for man but for the Lord God. So I have provided for the house of my God, so far as I was able, the gold for the things of gold, the silver for the things of silver, and the bronze for the things of bronze, the iron for the things of iron, and wood for the things of wood, besides great quantities of onyx and stones for setting, antimony, colored stones, all sorts of precious stones and marble. Moreover, in addition to all that I have provided for the holy house, I have a treasure of my own of gold and silver, and because of my devotion to the house of my God I give it to the house of my God: 3,000 talents of gold, of the gold of Ophir, and 7,000 talents of refined silver, for overlaying the walls of the house, ... 6 Then the leaders of fathers' houses made their freewill offerings, as did also the leaders of the tribes, the commanders of thousands and of hundreds, and the officers over the king's work. 7 They gave for the service of the house of God 5,000 talents and 10,000 darics of gold, 10,000 talents of silver, 18,000 talents of bronze, and 100,000 talents of iron." (1 Chronicles 29:1-7)

King David personally gave 3000 talents of gold, valued at about US$ 6 billion in 2024. In addition, his household gave almost twice as much. The total value of the gold alone is estimated at US$ 16 billion in 2024 value. Silver, bronze, iron, precious stones, wood,

94

fabrics, and spices are extra. David and his family were shepherds, and the core people around David were considered the distressed, the debtor, and the discontented.

"And everyone who was in distress, everyone who was in debt, and everyone who was discontented gathered to him." (1 Samuel 22:2)

God also reminded King David of his humble beginning as a shepherd, the youngest among his brothers, and made him the king of Israel.

"You must tell my servant David, 'This is what the Lord All-Powerful says: I took you from the pasture and from tending the sheep and made you leader of my people Israel. 9 I have been with you everywhere you have gone and have defeated your enemies for you. I will make you as famous as any of the great people on the earth. (2 Samuel 7:8-9)

God has prospered David and the people around him, to be the financier and the builder of the second dwelling place of God that is more glorious than the first one. God did it through a Wealth Transfer from the unrighteous to the righteous.

Prophecy of the New Testament Wealth Transfer

The prophet Isaiah prophesied about the Wealth Transfer in Isaiah 60 at about 700 BC. The previous chapters discussed the details of the prophecy. In around 500 BC, during the reign of King Cyrus in Persia, the prophet Haggai was involved with Zerubbabel in the reconstruction of the ruined Temple of Solomon after the destruction by King Nebuchadnezzar of Babylon. He also prophesied about "another" temple in the future.

"For thus says the LORD of hosts: 'Once more (it is a little while) I will shake heaven and earth, the sea and dry land; and I will shake all nations, and they shall come to (with) the desire (wealth) of all nations, and I will fill this temple with glory,' says the LORD of hosts. 'The silver is Mine, and the gold is Mine,' says the LORD of hosts. 'the glory of this latter temple shall be greater than the former,' says the LORD of hosts. 'And in this place I will give peace,' says the LORD of hosts." (Haggai 2:6-9)

The prophet Haggai prophesied of a future temple that will be filled with His glory. The glory of the future ("the latter") temple will be greater than the "former" temple, referring to the temple of Solomon. He also prophesied that God will give "peace" (Hb: shalom) in this temple. Jewish scholars and some Christians believe that the prophecy is about the "third temple" that is to be built at the same location as the Temple of Solomon – the same temple that was later rebuilt by Zerubbabel during the time of King Cyrus, and by king Herod the Great after the destruction by the Seleucids. The temple that existed during Jesus' life on the earth was finally destroyed to the ground by the Roman Emperor Titus in 70 AD. The dream of the Orthodox Jews to rebuild another temple may have created a major religious war. This is because, at the same location, an Ottoman Empire sultan built the Al Aqsa Mosque with the Dome of the Rock in the centre of it. This mosque is considered the third holiest site in Islam.

I do not believe that Haggai prophesied the third "physical" temple on earth. I believe God allowed the temple in Jerusalem to be destroyed in 70 AD as a sign that the Old Covenant of the Law was finished. Without a temple and its altar, the utensils for performing sacrifices, and without the Holy of Holies and the Ark of Covenant, nobody can perform all the Levitical offerings, especially the Sin Offering and the Burnt Offering. Therefore, the "so-called" redemption of sins cannot be performed anymore. Jesus Christ has completed His perfect work and fulfilled the requirement of the Law once and for all. The Old Covenant of the Law has become obsolete and must go away. Then, what kind of temple is the prophet Haggai referring to?

Fulfillment of The Prophecy

Christ, the Word, who is God, was reincarnated as a "man" to redeem mankind from sin and death. I will not dive into the Gospel of Grace deeper in this chapter because it is not the primary objective of the chapter. The grace of God has not only saved us through the forgiveness of sins and liberating us from the punishment and the curses due to sins and trespasses against the Law, but it has also restored us according to the plan of God from the beginning. We have discussed this in the previous chapters.

Luke, in the Book of Acts, describes the "temple" prophesied by Haggai. This is a "temple" that will not be made by men.

"God, who made the world and everything in it, since He is Lord of heaven and earth, does not dwell in temples made with hands." *(Acts 17:24)*

Later, the apostle Paul gave a more detailed description of the "temple" prophesied by Haggai.

"For you are the temple of the living God. As God has said: "I will dwell in them and walk among them. I will be their God, and they shall be My people." *(2 Corinthians 6:16)*

"Do you not know that you are the temple of God and that the Spirit of God dwells in you?" *(1 Corinthians 3:16)*

The believers in Christ, the New Testament Church, are the temple of the living God, where God is dwelling now - permanently. The apostle Peter added that every individual believer is a "living stone", an important part needed to build the House of God.

"Coming to Him as to a living stone, rejected indeed by men, but chosen by God and precious, you also, as living stones, are being built up a spiritual house, a holy priesthood, to offer up

spiritual sacrifices acceptable to God through Jesus Christ." (1 Peter 2:4)

Mega Construction Project to Build the Eternal Dwelling Place of God

God has been working on a Mega Construction Project to build His Eternal Dwelling Place for the past 2000 years. The apostles and the prophets are the "foundation", and Jesus Christ Himself is the "chief cornerstone".

"Now, therefore, you are no longer strangers and foreigners, but fellow citizens with the saints and members of the household of God, having been built on the foundation of the apostles and prophets, Jesus Christ Himself being the chief cornerstone, in whom the whole building, being fitted together, grows into a holy temple in the Lord, in whom you also are being built together for a dwelling place of God in the Spirit." (Ephesians 2:19-22)

Every day – for the past 2000 years - more "living stones" are added piece by piece. In the time of Acceleration, during the Great Harvest, we will see an increasing activity to complete the construction. I look forward to witnessing the completion. Every believer is invited and encouraged to take part in prayer, time, efforts, and also finances.

CHAPTER 6

THE PURPOSE OF WEALTH

A multitude of camels shall cover you,

the young camels of Midian and Ephah;

all those from Sheba shall come.

They shall bring gold and frankincense,

and shall bring good news, the praises of the Lord.

All the flocks of Kedar shall be gathered to you;

the rams of Nebaioth shall minister to you;

they shall come up with acceptance on my altar,

and I (God) will beautify my beautiful house. ...

Foreigners shall build up your walls,

and their kings shall minister to you;

for in my wrath I struck you,

but in my favor I have had mercy on you.

Your gates shall be open continually;

day and night they shall not be shut,

that people may bring to you the wealth of the nations,

with their kings led in procession.

For the nation and kingdom

that will not serve you shall perish;

those nations shall be utterly laid waste.

The glory of Lebanon shall come to you,

the cypress, the plane, and the pine,

to beautify the place of my sanctuary,

and I will make the place of my feet glorious. (Isaiah 60:6-13)

The Wealth of God

Mega Construction Project Requires Mega Resources

I have been in the building material business for many years. Though I am not involved in the construction project myself, I have been doing business with many contractors and builders – from design and planning to completion. Resources, such as materials and labours, are needed, but at the end of the day, it all comes down to the money required to complete the project. In his book "The Great Wealth Transfer," Peter Youngren wrote, *"God always provides the resources for His dwelling place"*. What an assurance! He will prosper His people through businesses, services, and works so that they can contribute to the Mega Construction Project. Christians have been giving to the church through tithe and offerings since the beginning of the church. If we read the prophecies of the Wealth Transfer in *Isaiah 60* and *Haggai 2*, God has planned for another avenue in providing finances for His Mega Construction Project in the End Time.

Isaiah 60:6-7 describes that the foreigners, signifying non-believers, will come on their camels, a picture of transportation vehicles, to bring gold and frankincense, very precious commodities, to the people of God. What attracted the non-believers to come will be the glory of the Lord and the light of God that are so visible inside the believers. They will also come with lots of flocks and rams, which are necessary to offer sacrifices to the LORD at the altar. Though the people of God may enjoy the wealth, we need to understand the primary purpose of the "wealth" brought to us? They are needed to *"beautify"* the House of God and to *"worship"* God in His house. That's the primary purpose of the Great Wealth Transfer.

View on Money

In the first chapter of this book, I have addressed briefly God's perspective on money. There will be a deeper discussion on *"Kingdom Finances"* in my future books. To comprehend the topic of the book, I would like to dive deeper into the issue of money. The apostle Paul and his supporters and co-workers, Priscilla and Aquila, were tent-makers. They were business people who had income to support themselves and their ministries. They have never asked for money for their own needs and also for their ministries. All the contributions went directly to the people who had dire needs. I admire their approach toward ministry and would like to be a "tent-maker" minister, too.

With regards to the purpose of money, the apostle Paul wrote in *2 Corinthians 9:6-8, 10-11), **"But this I say: He who sows sparingly will also reap sparingly, and he who sows bountifully will also reap bountifully. So let each one give as he purposes in his heart, not grudgingly or of necessity; for God loves a cheerful giver. And God is able to make all grace abound toward you, that you, always having all sufficiency in all things, may have an abundance for every good work. ... Now may He who supplies seed to the sower, and bread for food, supply and multiply the seed you*** *have sown and increase the fruits of your righteousness, 11 while you are enriched in everything for all liberality, which causes thanksgiving through us to God."*

He viewed money as seeds. Part of the seeds God supplied to us is to make bread to eat and live. The other part of the seeds is to be sown or invested, but we are investing in our Father's business. Investment in our business or the world's financial system requires ideas and executions. Investment in the Father's business also requires the same. God supplies all the seeds – the initial capital, ideas, the planning, the execution – more importantly, the environment that causes multiplication. God may not send a rain of money from the sky, though He could, but He has given us the power or ability and the circumstances to create wealth. This is according to His covenanted promise for God's people in the Old Testament and continued to God's people in the New Testament. The Bible says, *"And you shall remember the Lord your God, for it is He who gives you power to get wealth, that He may establish His covenant which He swore to your fathers, as it is this day."* *(Deuteronomy 8:18)*

The "simple" principle in investing is that the more seeds you sow, the more harvest you will reap. Every businessman, even if you put your money in the bank, will understand this principle. He also added that every farmer sows seeds cheerfully because he expects a bountiful harvest instead of with grudges because he sees it as a loss.

We are cheerful because we expect a return on our investment. God loves those who sow with cheerful expectation, knowing that God is the source of his sufficiency, even to the overflow. Jesus spoke on the subject of money more than any other subject in the Bible, including healing. Why? Jesus knew that *"the love of money. For the love of money is a root of all kinds of evil"* – not the money itself is evil.

Money is only a currency or tool for doing business, including the investment in our Father's business. The Bible told the Parable of Talents and the Parable of Minas, explaining the purpose of investing to receive a good return on our investment. The Bible also told the Parable of the Unrighteous Steward or Manager, which is the most misunderstood parable in the Bible. We are told to be as shrewd or wise or have the right judgment as that unrighteous steward. It is a picture of how we should view money and use it the correct way. We are to use the money that is not ours in the first place for the purpose of making friends in heaven. In another word, God is telling us to invest His money to bring more people to heaven – as our friends. The Father's business is to bring as many people to His kingdom as we can. In the Mega Construction context, we are to use His money to create more "living stones" to build His eternal dwelling place.

The apostle Paul called this attitude and action *"good work"* because this is according to the purpose of God. The opposite is

"Dead work" - doing things to receive God's acceptance with the expectation of the blessing of God – something that God has already given us abundantly. We do not work to get the blessing. We are blessed already, and we are expected to be an investor or a sower. The more seeds you sow, you can expect more increase in the fruits of your righteousness. What are the fruits of your righteousness? On one side, they are the glory of God in you, something that other people will see in you. The fruits of your righteousness are also the spread of righteousness, which is the gift of God to other people. More people will become *"the righteousness of God in Christ Jesus"*, thus the living stones for the House of God.

The Great Commission

After Jesus died and was resurrected, Jesus gave His disciples a very important command, often called the Great Commission. We can read the accounts in the Gospel of Mark and the Gospel of Matthew.

And He said to them, "Go into all the world and preach the gospel to every creature. He who believes and is baptized will be saved; but he who does not believe will be condemned. And these signs will follow those who believe: In My name they will cast out demons; they will speak with new tongues; they will take up serpents; and if they drink anything deadly, it will by no means

hurt them; they will lay hands on the sick, and they will recover."
(Mark 16:15-18)

*And Jesus came and said to them, "All authority in heaven
and on earth has been given to me. Go therefore and make
disciples of all nations, baptizing them in the name of the Father
and of the Son and of the Holy Spirit, teaching them to observe all
that I have commanded you. And behold, I am with you always, to
the end of the age." (Matthew 28:18-20)*

His instruction cannot be clearer than this. His command is
based on His desire to complete the Mega Construction project by
converting all the "dead stones" into the "living stones", and
bringing them into the construction site and using them to build
God's House, His Eternal Dwelling Place. He does not want any
stone left out, but He wants all stones from all nations or tribes to be
part of His Eternal Dwelling Place. He will not stop until all nations
have been given the opportunity to become a part of His house. Once
the Mega Construction Project is completed, then the end will come.
*JESUS CHRIST WILL RETURN WHEN HIS DWELLING PLACE
IS COMPLETED*

*"And this gospel of the kingdom will be preached in all the
world as a witness to all the nations, and then the end will come."*
(Matthew 24:14)

CHAPTER 7

ARE WE THERE YET?

If you have little children and you are on a long journey in a car, you will often hear them asking, "Are we there yet?" Children are usually impatient, especially when they are expecting something good or when they are unhappy in their current situation. A few weeks before Christmas, many parents wrapped the gifts and put them under the Christmas tree. Children cannot wait until Christmas day to tear the wrapping papers. They will check the gifts, shake them and inspect them, hoping they can peek through the narrow gaps between the wrapping paper. Many Christians are like that with their hope for the promises of God, including being in the image of Christ with all His glory, his supernatural power and wisdom. They are often impatient with their growth, especially when they go through the process of discipline. With regard to God's promises, many Christians are uninformed or unaware of the promises of God because they have not been taught or they do not read their Bibles. Many are ignorant, thinking they are irrelevant or unimportant to their lives. Many who are told or taught do not believe the promises of God for their lives. However, I am speaking to those who know, believe and expect the fulfillment of the promises of God in their lives but are struggling and restless because they have waited expectantly for a long time and have not seen even *"a cloud of the size of a fist"*. Some may have seen that *"cloud"*, but are still waiting for the *"heavy rain"* to come.

Discerning The Time Seasons

For Christians who understand and believe in the *"hope of glory"*, the *"predestined"* promise of God, let us learn what to do next. God imparted different anointings to His people. In fact, I believe He wants us to have the fullness of God in Christ Jesus, including all His *"anointings"*. Let me explain the term anointing in a simple way. The act of anointing or being anointed in the Old Testament referred to being smeared or rubbed with oil as part of a ceremony to make someone or something sacred. John Maxwell defines anointing as **"God's intimate presence and enabling power."** *(Maxwell Leadership Bible, p 212)* God put each of us on earth to fulfill a specific purpose that He chose for us to fulfill. Jesus is Christ or Messiah, which means *"The Anointed One"*. He obeyed the will of the Father to the point of His death – that no one will perish, but he will be raised up on the last day. Os Guinness wrote in his book *"The Call"*, we all are called to the same *to* which is to become a person God planned to be through Jesus Christ. Because we are in Christ, we are all *"the anointed ones"* – to be imitators of Christ. He also wrote that everyone is also called to a *"Secondary Call"*, but it is specific for each person. When the Holy Spirit takes up residence inside us, He anoints us to do the work God has chosen or purposed us to do – the Primary and Secondary Calls.

There is specific anointing that some charismatic Christians call the *"Issachar Anointing"*. It is the anointing or the ability to understand and discern the time and seasons and to have wisdom on what to do with the information. The Issachar tribe used the information they acquired to advise the rest of Israel on what to do.

1 Chronicles 12:32 **... of the sons of Issachar who had understanding of the times, to know what Israel ought to do, their chiefs were two hundred; and all their brethren were at their command; ...**

Jesus pointed out to the Jews during His ministry on earth that there are people with such anointing among them to understand the weather. However, the leaders of the Jews – the Pharisees, the Scribes and the Sadducees – could not discern the *"time"* when Christ or the Messiah was in front of them. They were well versed in the prophecies in the Old Testament that pointed towards Jesus. They have seen the signs and wonders that fulfilled the prophecies, yet their hardened hearts prevented them from discerning the time that Messiah was already in front of them. Jesus rebuked them strongly for their lack of discernment.

Then He also said to the multitudes, "Whenever you see a cloud rising out of the west, immediately you say, 'A shower is coming'; and so it is. And when you see the south wind blow, you say, 'There will be hot weather'; and there is. Hypocrites! You can discern the face of the sky and of the earth, but how is it you do not discern this time? (Luke 12:54-56)

Seeing With Your Spiritual Eyes

Jesus warned the disciples not to be like the Jewish leaders of His time. He instructed them to *"see"*. I believe Jesus spoke to them about seeing in the spiritual realm with their spiritual eyes or the eyes of their hearts. The time is coming soon when the harvest is ready because the fields have become "white" due to the ripening "wheat".

John 4:35 Do you not say, 'There are yet four months, then comes the harvest'? Look, I tell you, lift up your eyes, and see that the fields are white for harvest.

I am asking you all, "Are you seeing the white field that is ready for harvest?" The apostle Paul prayed for the church of Ephesus that they would receive the Spirit of wisdom and revelation in the knowledge of Christ and that their hearts would be enlightened or seen.

I do not cease to give thanks for you, remembering you in my prayers, that the God of our Lord Jesus Christ, the Father of glory, may give you the Spirit of wisdom and of revelation in the knowledge of Him, having the eyes of your hearts enlightened, that you may know what is the hope to which he Has called you, what are the riches of His glorious inheritance in the saints, and what is the immeasurable greatness of His power toward us who believe, according to the working of His great might ... (Ephesians 1:16-19)

I am praying for all of you that the Father of glory will give you the Spirit of wisdom and the Spirit of revelation, and He will enlighten your spiritual eyes, the eyes of your hearts, that you may see and know the time we are in now, and know what to do.

The Great Harvest

I believe you are able to see now that the Great Harvest is here. Jesus told His disciples 2000 years ago, and He is still telling us that the labourers are few. He instructed us to pray earnestly, in collaboration with the Holy Spirit, that our Father, the Lord of the

Harvest, will send labourers to the field. *"And He said to them, "The harvest is plentiful, but the laborers are few. Therefore, pray earnestly to the Lord of the harvest to send out laborers into his harvest."* (Luke 10:2)

I pray that many of you who read this book will be touched and enlightened by the Holy Spirit and will respond to His calling. The apostle Paul clarified further the next steps:

"How then shall they call on Him in whom they have not believed? And how shall they believe in Him of whom they have not heard? And how shall they hear without a preacher? 15 And how shall they preach unless they are sent? As it is written: "How beautiful are the feet of those who preach the gospel of peace, who bring glad tidings of good things!" (Romans 10:14-15)

In Module 2 of the "Global Gospel Institute" course, Peter Youngren said that all churches must be involved in the preaching of the Gospel of Peace, or the Gospel of Grace. A church must do a minimum of two out of the three parts: **PRAY, SEND and GO**. If a church or a Christian, cannot go to share the Gospel to the unbelievers, especially to the people or the tribes who have never heard the Gospel, it shall, at least, pray for and send the workers. Sending can mean commissioning people to go., and providing resources, such as training and finances. I encourage all readers of this book to inquire about the Financial Reports of your church and find out how many percent of your church's income is used for the purpose of outreach, instead of internal operations, such as salaries and building funds.

All Are Called

Many Christians have excuses. Some would say, "I don't have the time", or "I don't have the money". Many would say, "I have not studied the Bible enough to preach the Gospel", or "I am just an engineer, an accountant, or a teacher", or "I don't know how to speak in public", or "I am too young", or "I am too old". Let us see what the apostle Paul considered *"qualified"*.

Where is the one who is wise? Where is the scribe? Where is the debater of this age? Has not God made foolish the wisdom of the world? ... For consider your calling, brothers: not many of you were wise according to worldly standards, not many were powerful, not many were of noble birth. But God chose what is foolish in the world to shame the wise; God chose what is weak in the world to shame the strong; God chose what is low and despised in the world, even things that are not, to bring to nothing things that are, so that no human being might boast in the presence of God. (1 Corinthians 1:20-29)

Everybody is qualified to be used by God. God often chooses unlikely people, the un-noble, the foolish, the weak, the lowly and despised, even the forgotten ones, like Moses. Moses was trained as a prince in the palace in all areas of government, economy, finances and warfare. He could have become a king of Egypt. However, at the age of 40, he made a mistake when he killed another Egyptian because he wanted to be the saviour of his people, Israel. He took matters into his own hands and did not wait for the LORD to open the door. He ended up spending the next 40 years of his life in the wilderness as a lowly shepherd. He was forgotten and irrelevant. Without knowing it, God used the second 40 years of his life as a training period for him to be humble and more willing to listen to God. At the age of 80, when he felt like a "has-been" or the "forgotten one", God chose him to liberate and lead the people of God out of Egypt to the Promised Land. God is faithful. Your calling is irrevocable regardless of time and situation. Moses became a stutterer with low self-esteem, and God had to choose Aaron to help him. However, God chose the same person He called before - for such an important task. If God chose an old "has-been" like Moses, he can choose any of you – as long as you are willing!

FINAL REMARK

This book tells the story of my journey, indirectly, since God found me 25 years ago, reconciled me to Himself, gave me a life – an abundant life, led me through a process of discipline out of His love for me, and took me on a journey of "hope of glory" that He had predestined even before I was even born. He truly had me *"Destined For Glory"*. I have never regretted what I had experienced—all my worldly credentials and wealth. I used to be proud of my sharp mind, human wisdom, PhD in engineering, and my once-successful company, *Nexwood.* Now, I consider them "nothing" compared to the richness and the fullness of Him in me and what is coming in the future. If I look back 25 years, I was "successful" in business and "respected" in my church circle due to my ministry and service, but I don't like who I was – a proud person with self-reliance and self-effort. The process of discipline, a glorification process that I went through and is still continuing until now, has changed me and will continue to change me for the better.

In my humble opinion, I saw a "very small" parallel between myself and the apostle Paul, a misguided but very accomplished scholar who encountered Christ Jesus and transformed his life radically. He became a businessman and tentmaker to support his financial needs, but his extraordinary ministry, driven and empowered by the Holy Spirit, determined who he was. He considered all that he had, including his top education that led him to be one of the Sanhedrin members and the Pharisee of all Pharisees, as "dung" compared to the opportunity to know Christ - the eternal life. His life was not easy. He was hated by His former friends, sanctified in the seclusion of the wilderness for years, and put in prison. The envious religious leaders plotted to kill him. He was ship-wrecked on the way to be judged and imprisoned in Rome. The exact details of the apostle Paul's death are unknown, but tradition holds that he was beheaded in Rome. He died as a martyr for his faith. He fought the good fight of faith, and he finished the race and received the imperishable crown. That's the glory of the Lord seen in him. I cannot see myself with such suffering for the glory of God, but I hope that people will see the glory of Jesus in me.

I have seen leaders, companies and organizations rise and fall. I have seen my own company rise and fall. I have been in the mountains and the valleys of life, but I can testify that God is faithful – even when I was faithless. My journey – I call it Journey to Glory

– has not been easy. But I am grateful that He took me through this journey. I know some people, including my wife, who think I am a better person: humbler and more patient. I really desire for others – Christians and unbelievers – to see the glory of Christ in me more and more. Though I would also like to have His wisdom, power, authority and dominion in me, I mostly desire to see His character, which is the fruit of the Spirit, within me.

I encourage all of you, Christians, to commit yourselves to take the path of the journey to glory. You are Destined For Glory. The hope of glory is worth the pain, the struggles, the dark periods of life and all the frustrations you may experience. If you are *"willing and obedient",* you will be glorified as God has promised.

As for you who have not known Christ and the Father and have not experienced the love and the grace of God, I pray that the Holy Spirit will open the eyes of your heart to see the great and wonderful plan of God for you. You are chosen. You are qualified. You are destined to glory. I hope you will decide to respond and say "Yes!" to His invitation to life and glory.

To God be the glory!